MERCEDES-BENZ 190 SL

1955-63

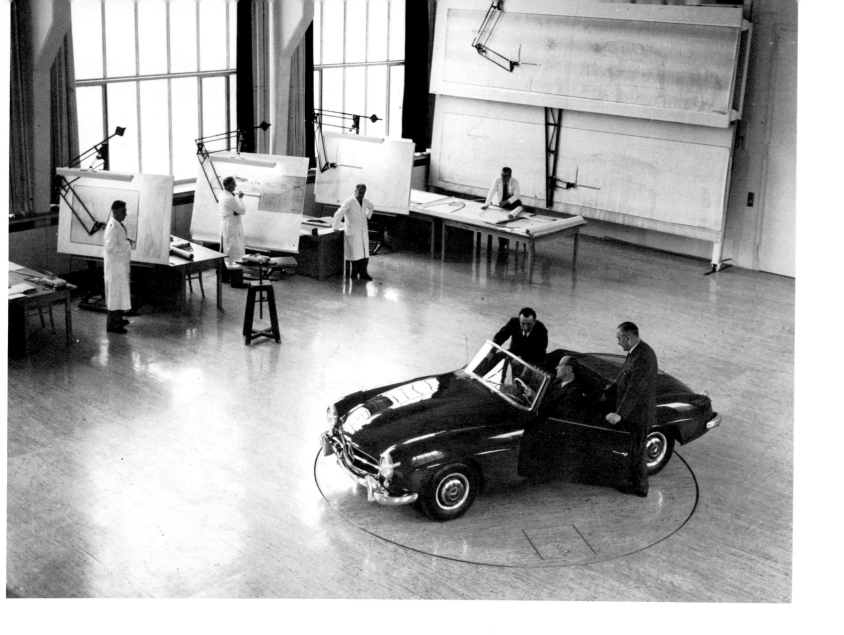

MERCEDES-BENZ 190 SL

1955-63

A Documentation by Walter Zeichner

1469 Morstein Road, West Chester, Pennsylvania 19380

This volume of the Schiffer Automotive Series is dedicated to the Mercedes-Benz 190 SL, a sporting two-seater built between 1955 and 1963 and still enjoying great popularity as a collector car today. This book is not intended to be a technically perfect reference book on the 190 SL by any means, nor a repair or restoration manual. The Schiffer Automotive Series are rather to be seen as picture books of automobile nostalgia, meant to take the observer back to a time that may not actually lie too far in the past, and yet is already history. Many of us still remember when the 190 SL was part of the everyday traffic scene.

We express our thanks to our helpful colleagues who assisted in gathering historical materials, particularly Georg Amtmann and Robert Horender, the latter of whom is also responsible for the model car data on page 84.

Halwart Schrader, Editor

Translated from the German by Dr. Edward Force.

Printed in the United States of America.
ISBN: 0-88740-209-7

Originally published under the title "Mercedes 190 SL", 1955-63, Schrader Motor Chronik, copyright Schrader Automobil-Bücher, Handels-GmbH, München, West Germany, © 1986, ISBN: 3-922617-14-X.

Published by Schiffer Publishing, Ltd.
1469 Morstein Road
West Chester, Pennsylvania 19380
Please write for a free catalog.
This book may be purchased from the publisher.
Please include $2.00 postage.
Try your bookstore first.

Contents

190 SL-A Car Lover's Car from the Start   6
The "Little Brother" of the 300 SL   10
The Favorite Competitors   72
The 190 SL in Miniature   84

The 190 SL as Seen in the Press   86
Technical Data   93
Mercedes-Benz Literature   94
Mercedes-Benz Clubs   94

190 SL-A Car Lover's Car from the Start

The firm of Daimler-Benz, whose significance in the history of the automobile needs no explanation, provided sports-minded people, especially between the two world wars with speedsters like the S-types, the 500 and 540 K, the roadsters of the 170, 290 and 320 series, automotive treasures that must remain a dream for most classic car fans today. The prices of such cars, when they come on the market at all, are practically equal to the cost of a luxurious one-family house.

Nonetheless, whomever enjoys a taste of the sporting past of that noble Swabian brand can look above all to the Type 190 SL. Built between 1955 and 1963, this vehicle provides definite references to the Type 300 SL, its older and mightier brother. With these two sports cars the era of truly sporty Mercedes cars came to an end, for their pagoda-roofed successors, down to the roadsters of today, cannot deny their somewhat limousine-like character.

In 1950 Daimler-Benz had already put on the market, in the coupe and convertible versions of the 170, 220 and 300 series, cars with a touch of sportiness but, in terms of their appearance, quite nostalgic vehicles for their prosperous clients in the early days of the Economic Miracle. In 1952 the 300 SL appeared on the world's racecourses, but until August of 1954 only a civil production version of this fascinating car, that radiated an almost brutal aura even while standing still, could be purchased.

This was changed, particularly by Max Hoffmann, the Mercedes importer for the United States, who anticipated good sales potential for such a sports car, since the American market at that time was a profitable area for the manufacturers of European sports cars.

But Hoffmann did not just successfully inspire the construction of the 300 SL series, he also considered it sensible to develop a smaller sports car with the euphonious name of Mercedes for young people and less prosperous enthusiasts, and was finally able to convince Daimler-Benz of the value of his idea. In January of 1954 the magazine *Auto, Motor und Sport* was already publishing drawings of the little sports car, though without knowing with what technical equipment the car would appear. Of course one could imagine that the short chassis of the new pontoon-type 180 would be made use of, but predictions favored a 1600 cc motor, and they soon proved to be wrong.

On February 6, 1954, on the occasion of the International Motor Sports Show, the 300 SL and 190 SL were presented to the public. It was clear to see that the 190 SL had been planned as the little brother of the already famous 300 SL, for much stress had been put on very similar styling. But the 190 SL was considerably more graceful than its bullish big brother, despite the same elements of style. The front sections of the two cars differed only in that the hood of the 300 SL came down lower and the transition from the 190 SL's fenders to its hood was more gentle. The prototype, in fact, still had an air inlet, and the 300 SL's hood was adorned with two bulges. Over the car's front wheel wells, the long spray deflectors, so characteristic of the 300 SL, had been modeled. Just as with the 300 SL, they had dared to do without the traditional Mercedes radiator grille, and so the 190 SL also inhaled its cool air through a wide "mouth" decorated with a single large Star of Stuttgart.

At the same time a version called the "Sport-roadster" was announced, intended for the drivers who wanted to use the car mainly for racing. These cars had only a small plexiglass windshield on the driver's side instead of the full windshield that curved gently to the sides, and side doors of light metal with deep cutouts into which small crank-operated windows were built.

Whereas the 300 SL could be purchased immediately after its showing, more then a year was to pass before the 190 SL could brighten up the road scene. During this time a few changes were made to the car, and an even greater similarity to the 300 SL was attained. In the production car, the air scoop on the motor hood was replaced by a central arch, and this was shortened considerably, so that it didn't quite reach the radiator grille, rather ending, as on the 300 SL, a good hand's-breadth short of it. The 190 SL now also had the long spray deflectors over its rear wheel wells. The front bumper, like that of the 300 SL, now followed the curves of the front body, and even the directional light housings followed the great pattern, being round instead of squarish. The motor of the car, which went into production in May of 1955, had been developed from the overhead cam type, introduced in 1951, which powered the 220 and 300 sedans. To be sure, two cylinders had been dropped from the six-cylinder motor, and the stroke had been shortened by 4.4 mm. The overhead camshaft of this motor was driven by the crankshaft via a duplex roller chain with automatic tension, and two Solex double carburetors supplied the powerplant with a mixture of fuel and air.

This motor, with 8.5:1 compression, produced 105 DIN horsepower at 5700 rpm and a maximum torque of 14.5 mKg. The motor had originally had somewhat more power, but for series production the decision was made to throttle it down a bit. With the

7

exception of a slight increase of the compression ratio to 8.8:1, which did not, however, make for an increase in performance, no essential changes were made to the powerplant package to the end of 190 SL's production life in 1963.

The car's bodywork was welded and self-bearing, with the so-called frame-bottom layout, its construction type taken from the Type 180, which had been revolutionary for Daimler-Benz. The front axle, with the motor and fully synchronized four-speed gearbox, with the sporty central shift lever, formed a completely demountable sub-chassis; the front wheels were individually mounted on double-wishbone transverse links with central coil springs and telescopic oleopneumatic shock absorbers. In the rear of the sports car, the single-joint swing axle, thoroughly proved in racing, offered its services. Duplex brakes at the front provided even slowing, and all the aluminum brake drums were finned for

better cooling (turbo-ventilation). Power brakes provided by ATE, at first available only optionally, became standard equipment as of May 1956.

From the beginning the 190 SL was available as a folding-top convertible or a coupe with a light metal hardtop and somewhat nobler decor. However, one could easily convert the convertible to a coupe with the hardtop too. The doors and seats of the coupe were covered in genuine leather as standard equipment, available in the convertible only at a higher price. The seats of the open car were of the bucket type and were equipped with seat cushions, while the coupe had upholstered seats of which only the backs folded, while the convertible's entire seats folded forward. A transverse spare seat for the small luggage space behind the seats was available as an extra, so that a third person could be carried (more roughly than rightly).

Above: A 1954 prototype. The hardtop (far left) is still from the first series, with the small rear window. At left: the motor of the 190 SL.

The roadster's top was made of heavy canvas and stood out in terms of exact fit and easy handling. Though the 190 SL was at first available only in silver gray, this changed in the 1957 model year, when a colorful choice of hues for the paintwork and interior became available; the folding top too, that previously had always been black, could be ordered in suitable shades.

Whoever valued it and did not mind the cost could also order a set of luggage made to fit the dimensions of the luggage space and trunk exactly, and offer maximum space utilization. The dashboard was richly appointed by contemporary standards, with a large speedometer and tachometer as well as oil pressure, water temperature and fuel gauges. As of 1959 a clock also decorated the lid of the glove compartment.

For the 190 SL, of which 25,881 were built from May of 1955 to February of 1963, there were essentially no changes.

In September of 1959 the coupe's top was provided with a rear window that curved well around the sides.

From the beginning, Daimler-Benz tried to give the car the image of a "touring sports car", to differentiate it from its rawboned competitors of the Triumph TR 3 or Alfa Romeo Giulietta Spider type. When one sits down in the 190 SL, one certainly feels that one is in a real sports car, though this impression of the thoroughbred is contradicted by the big steering wheel. In its time, too, the car was not only praised, but often unjustly measured by its big brother, the 300 SL, with which it showed no trace of similarity in terms of performance and handling. The motor, inherently quite lively, ran rough and loud at medium speeds, and the suspension was more suited to the demands of a sedan, despite giving the car very good roadholding. The little SL, with its almost 1.2-ton weight, also put a good deal of weight on the wheels, which made the car work hard to reach even the 170-kph mark.

But even a price of DM 16,500 for the roadster and 17,650 for the coupe with hardtop and folding top did not hurt the sales success of the 190 SL (especially in the USA). Whoever wanted a touring car that looked sporty and could also satisfy certain demands in terms of comfort was a potential customer of the Daimler-Benz firm.

Whoever thinks about buying a 190 SL today will expect to pay at least twice what the car cost when new. But if one is lucky enough to find a good specimen, which is not easy considering the car's popularity, one can have the pleasure of driving a car that is fascinating despite its minor weaknesses, alluring in its first-class workmanship and enjoyable comfort, and above all, a car that lets one enjoy top-down driving in its nicest form.

Auf allen Rennstrecken.

auf denen die sieggewohnten Wagen mit dem weltberühmten Mercedes-Benz-Stern führen, haben die Konstrukteure der Daimler-Benz Aktiengesellschaft ihre Erfahrungen gesammelt. Alles, was der Weiterentwicklung dienen konnte, wurde auf den großen internationalen Rennen der härtesten Prüfung unterzogen.

Anpassungsfähig an die Wünsche seines Besitzers und bei aller Verwandelbarkeit immer gleich elegant und von bestechender Schönheit, ist der 190 SL der ideale Wagen für alle Automobilisten, die im Hinblick auf Technik und Ästhetik hohe Ansprüche an ihr Fahrzeug stellen.

Ob Sie Ihren Wagen auf täglicher Fahrt im Stadtverkehr oder auf Reisen benutzen wollen, ob Sie bei schönem Wetter das „offene Fahren" lieben oder die repräsentative Note eines geschlossenen Wagens bevorzugen — der Typ 190 SL erfüllt in seiner Vielseitigkeit noch mehr als diese Wünsche.

Die serienmäßige Ausf... silbergrauer metallic-L... Spezialsitzen, die wahlw... blauem, creme oder gru... geliefert werden, bietet... ein versenkbares Verdeck... senkbare Seitenscheiben a... lichkeiten eines echten Ro... Für sportliches Fahren las... Türen gegen leichte Seiten... Armausschnitt und die Wir... scheibe gegen eine vor dem... angebrachte kleine Sportsch... Plexiglas austauschen. Zur... Gewichtsminderung können... dem das Verdeck und die Sto... abgenommen werden.
Durch Aufsetzen eines auf So... wunsch lieferbaren Daches wi... Typ 190 SL Roadster zum Co... das gediegene Eleganz mit völ... Witterungsunempfindlichkeit... verbindet.
Hohe Leistung und imponieren... Fahreigenschaften geben dem T... 190 SL seinen sportlichen Charak... während der für einen Touren-Sp... wagen außergewöhnliche Raum-... und Fahrkomfort, seine zeitsparer... Schnelligkeit und Wirtschaftlichke... dem 190 SL alle Merkmale eines vo... züglichen Gebrauchsfahrzeugs geb...

Neben dem sieggewohnten 300 SL ist auch der neue Typ 190 SL mit seinen überragenden Eigenschaften ein vorbildliches Beispiel für den Wert der Rennerfahrung in ihrer Anwendung auf den Serienfahrzeugbau.

Coupé mit Leichtmetalldach und Polstersitzen aus echtem Leder. Nach Lösen der innen angebrachten Verschlüsse ist das Dach abzunehmen und offen zu fahren oder gegen ein auf Sonderwunsch lieferbares Roadster-Verdeck austauschbar.

Three Wishes-Fulfilled with One Car!

Three wishes are fulfilled by the Mercedes 190 SL, says this 1956 brochure. The three varieties: coupe, roadster and racing sports car, were meant. The last, though, remained a rarity-this 190 hardly ever appeared on the racetracks here. The 190 SL was a "sporty" car, though, even though a comparison with the 300 SLR (upper left) was not completely realistic.

it einem Wagen erfüllt

Für sportliches Fahren
auf Sonderwunsch mit Sporttüren aus Leichtmetall
und Sportscheibe

Zur weiteren Gewichtsverminderung
können die Stoßstangen und auch das
Verdeck abgeschraubt werden

On all racecourses, on which the victorious cars with the world-famous Mercedes-Benz Star have run, the constructors of the Daimler-Benz Corporation have gathered their experience. Everything that could serve further development was put to the hardest tests in great international races.

Along with the victorious 300 SL, the new Type 190 SL, with its excellent qualities, is a shining example of the value of racing experience in its application to production car construction.

Adaptable to the wishes of its owner and equally elegant and bewitchingly beautiful in all its forms, the 190 SL is the ideal car for all motorists who have high requirements in terms of their car's technology and esthetics.

Whether you want to use your car for daily driving in city traffic or on trips, whether you love "top-down driving" in nice weather or prefer the serious tone of a closed car-the Type 190 SL fulfills more than these wishes through its versatility.

Coupe with light metal roof and upholstered seats in genuine leather. After loosening the attachments inside the car, the roof can be removed for open-air driving or exchanged for an optionally available convertible top.

The series production version with metallic silver-gray paint and special seats in your choice of blue, cream or green leatherette, offers you all the pleasures of a genuine roadster with its lowering top and side windows. For sporting driving the doors can be exchanged for light side-doors with cutouts and the windshield for a small sport shield of plexiglas mounted in front of the driver. For further weight reduction, the convertible top and the bumpers can be removed.

By mounting an optionally available roof, the Type 190 SL Roadster becomes a coupe that blends well-bred elegance with complete weather-tightness.

High performance and impressive driving qualities give the Type 190 SL its sporting character, while the space and driving comfort, extraordinary for a touring sports car, plus its time-saving speed and economy, give the 190 SL all the characteristics of an outstandingly useful car.

... fulfilled with one car

Roadster with fully lowering top of rubberized fabric, large watertight rear window sewn into the top.

For sporty driving sport-type light metal doors and sport windshield are available optionally.

For further weight reduction, the bumpers as well as the top can be detached.

A 1954 brochure page already portrays a prototype of the 190 SL as a long-awaited sports car. Only in November of 1955 did the already long-awaited 190 SL go into production. Here is the first brochure, intended to make clear its relationship to racing sports cars.

11

Kraft und Tempo - leicht beherrscht

Zweckvolle Schönheit zeichnet auch das elegant geschwungene Armaturenbrett des Typ 190 SL aus. Unbesorgt kann sein Besitzer im starken Stadtverkehr fahren oder sich dem Genuß einer sportlich-zügigen Fahrt hingeben. Die übersichtliche Anordnung aller Instrumente und die spielend leichte Betätigung der Bedienungsorgane lassen ihn jederzeit seinen schnellen Wagen mühelos beherrschen. Ungehindert kann die Straße über die flache Kühlerhaube bis kurz vor den Wagen eingesehen werden. Scheibenwischer mit zwei Geschwindigkeiten und breiten, sich überschneidenden Wischfeldern sorgen stets für klare Sicht durch die große, gewölbte Windschutzscheibe, während eine breite Sonnenblende den Fahrer gegen zu starke Lichteinwirkung schützt.

Direkt im Blickfeld des Fahrers liegen blendfrei angeordnet die beiden wichtigsten Instrumente dieses sportlichen Fahrzeugs – der Tachometer mit Gesamt- und Tageskilometerzähler sowie der Drehzahlmesser. Darunter sind Ölmanometer, Fernthermometer und Kraftstoffmesser sowie sämtliche Kontrollanzeigen in sinnvoll durchdachter Gruppierung zusammengefaßt. Die untere Kante des Armaturenbretts ist mit Texleder bezogen. Von oben reicht ebenfalls ein blendfreier Texleder-Überzug bis an den Rand der Instrumententafel, die alles enthält, was neben der Beherrschung des temperamentvollen Wagens dem Fahrkomfort dient – wie die Hebel der für beide Vordersitze getrennt regulierbaren Heizung und Belüftung, den geräumigen Handschuhkasten, den Zigarrenanzünder und Ascher, die abblendbare Innenleuchte und außerdem Raum für das auf Sonderwunsch eingebaute Autoradio.

Breite, verschließbare Türen

machen das Ein- und Aussteigen bequem und bieten mit Druckknopfbetätigung, Kurbelfenstern und großen, als Zuggriff und Armlehne ausgebildeten Türtaschen die beim Tourenwagen gewohnten Annehmlichkeiten.

Die Sporttüren aus Leichtmetall

auf Sonderwunsch gegen Mehrpreis geben mit ihren vertieften Armausschnitten dem Typ 190 SL die beim sportlichen Fahren gewünschte Gewichtsverminderung.

Wide locking doors make getting in and out easy, and offer the conveniences one is accustomed to in touring cars: push-button door handles, lowering windows, and big door pockets formed as handles and armrests.

Purposeful beauty is also shown in the elegant lines of the Type 190 SL's dashboard. Its owner can drive carefree in heavy city traffic or enjoy the pleasures of a sporty fast ride. The readily visible arrangement of all the instruments and the playfully easy operation of the controls let him control his fast car easily at all times. Without obstruction, the road can be seen over the flat motor hood to a short distance in front of the car. Windshield wipers with two speeds and wide, overlapping blades always provide a clear view through the big arched windshield, while a broad sun visor protects the driver from the effect of too-bright light.

Directly in the driver's field of vision, arranged to be glare-free, are the two most important instruments of this sports car-the speedometer with total and daily odometers, and the tachometer. Below them are the oil pressure gauge, engine thermometer and fuel gauge, plus all the control indicators, organized in sensibly planned groups. The lower edge of the dashboard is covered in leatherette. On the top a likewise non-glare leatherette covering extend to the edge of the instrument panel, which includes everything that serves not only the control of the lively car but also your riding comfort-like the lever for the separate regulation of heating and ventilation of the two front seats, the roomy glove compartment, the cigarette lighter and ashtray, the non-glare interior lights, as well as space for the optionally installed auto radio.

The sport doors of light metal optionally available at an additional price, give the Type 190 SL the weight decrease wanted for sporting driving through their deep cutouts.

The dashboard of the Mercedes-Benz 190 SL radiates the refined elegance of a typical luxury car from Stuttgart. In this catalog there is also a reference to the "Sportroadster", which was built in very small numbers but hardly ever raced ...

MERCEDES-BENZ

Typ 190 SL

MERCEDES-BENZ

Zwei Wagen in einem

vereinigen sich in dem neuen Mercedes-Benz-Tourensportwagen Typ 190 SL. Als Reisewagen wie für die tägliche Fahrt im Stadtverkehr bietet der rassig-elegante zweisitzige Roadster für einen Wagen sportlichen Charakters ein ungewöhnlich hohes Maß von Fahrkomfort, Zuverlässigkeit und Sicherheit. Zeitsparende Schnelligkeit und Geräumigkeit, Wirtschaftlichkeit und leichte Bedienung machen ihn zum vorzüglichen Gebrauchsfahrzeug. Darüber hinaus ermöglichen seine hohe Leistung und imponierenden Fahreigenschaften die erfolgreiche Teilnahme an motorsportlichen Wettbewerben.

Die reichen Daimler-Benz-Erfahrungen im Renn- und Sportwagenbau und die jüngsten Erkenntnisse moderner Personenwagen-Konstruktionen sichern dem neuen Roadster die markanten Vorzüge, die bei allen Anforderungen eindrucksvoll den Begriff „Mercedes-Benz-Sicherheit" beweisen.

Ganz nach Ihren Wünschen

können Sie alle Annehmlichkeiten eines komfortablen Reisewagens genießen oder die kraftvolle Schnelligkeit des Typ 190 SL nach äußerlicher Veränderung im sportlichen Einsatz ausnutzen. Während bei der Normalausstattung ein versenkbares, ohne jede Mühe bedienbares Verdeck und versenkbare Seitenscheiben die Annehmlichkeiten eines echten Roadsters bieten, lassen sich für sportliche Veranstaltungen die Türen gegen leichte Seitentüren mit Armausschnitt und die Windschutzscheibe gegen einen nur vor dem Fahrer angebrachten Schutzschild aus Plexiglas austauschen. Zur weiteren Gewichtsverminderung können außerdem Verdeck und Stoßstangen abgenommen werden.

Die geräumigen Taschen an den breiten Türen sind oben mit einem langgestreckten Wulst versehen, der gleichzeitig als Armstütze und Zugriff dient

In der Formschönheit und Harmonie der Linien spiegelt sich echte Sindelfinger Karosserie-Baukunst. Die niedere Motorhaube gewährt hervorragende Sicht auf die Fahrbahn bis unmittelbar vor den Wagen und einen guten Blick über die Kotflügel. Fahrkomfort und Ausstattung bestätigen die glückliche Verbindung von sportlicher Note und Leistung mit der Bequemlichkeit des Reisewagens. Die eingebaute Lüftung und Heizung, auf jeder Seite getrennt regulierbar, sorgt stets für ein angenehmes Klima. Spielend leicht zu bedienende Lenkung und Schaltung sowie eine Fülle kleiner Annehmlichkeiten von der Druckknopftüröffnung bis zur Leselampe machen jeden Kilometer in dem schmucken sportlichen Roadster zur Freude.

Sicheren Halt

und bequemen Sitz bei jeder Fahrweise geben die für diesen schnellen Wagen entwickelten Spezialsitze. Sie sind in Längsrichtung verstellbar und können nach vorn umgeklappt werden. Außerdem kann im Fond ein dritter Sitz – quer zur Fahrtrichtung – angebracht werden.

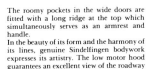

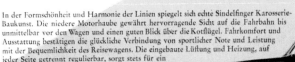

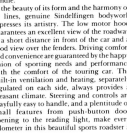

Two Cars in One are blended in the new Mercedes-Benz Type 190 SL touring sports car. For long trips as for daily driving in heavy traffic, the refined and elegant two-seat roadster offers an unbelievably high degree of riding comfort for a car of sporting character. Time-saving speed and roominess, economy and easy service make it an excellent utility vehicle. Beyond that, its high performance and imposing handling characteristics make possible its successful participation in motor-sporting events.

The wealth of Daimler-Benz experience in racing and sports car construction and the most recent experience in passenger car construction assure the new roadster the significant advantages that impressively assure the concept of "Mercedes-Benz safety" under all conditions.

Exactly as you wish you can enjoy all the conveniences of a comfortable touring car or utilize the powerful quickness of the Type 190 SL after external changes for sporting use. While in its normal state a lowering top, operable without any trouble, and lowering side windows offer the advantages of a real roadster, the doors can be exchanged for light side doors with cutouts, and the windshield for a protective plexiglas shield just in front of the driver, for sporting events. For further weight reduction, the top and bumpers can also be removed.

A safe hold and a comfortable seat in every type of driving are given by the special seats developed for this fast car. They are adjustable longitudinally and can be folded forward. In addition, a third seat can be installed transversely in the rear.

The roomy pockets in the wide doors are fitted with a long ridge at the top which simultaneously serves as an armrest and handle.

In the beauty of its form and the harmony of its lines, genuine Sindelfingen bodywork expresses its artistry. The low motor hood guarantees an excellent view of the roadway to a short distance in front of the car and a good view over the fenders. Driving comfort and convenience are guaranteed by the happy union of sporting needs and performance with the comfort of the touring car. The built-in ventilation and heating, separately regulated on each side, always provides a pleasant climate. Steering and controls are playfully easy to handle, and a plentitude of small features from push-button door opening to the reading light, make every kilometer in this beautiful sports roadster a joy.

1955

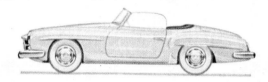

190 SL

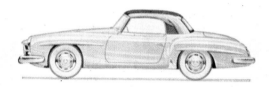

As the "little brother of the 300 SL", the 190 SL looked very attractive with the sporty seats and other attributes of the "big boy".

Naturally, advertisements for the 190 SL appeared in respected automobile journals.

AS COUPE OR ROADSTER

perfected in either form
Whether you drive the 190 SL as a roadster or turn it into a coupe by installing the metal roof-what the perfected form of its bodywork makes evident in dynamic verve, makes for an inspiring experience for you at the wheel of this spirited car.

Your lucky star on all roads—MERCEDES-BENZ

in jeder Form vollendet

Ob Sie den 190 SL als Roadster fahren

oder ihn durch das aufsetzbare Metalldach in ein Coupé verwandeln -

was die vollendete Form seiner Karosserie an dynamischem Schwung erkennen läßt.

wird für Sie am Steuer dieses temperamentvollen Wagens zu einem begeisternden Erlebnis.

IHR GUTER STERN AUF ALLEN STRASSEN

MERCEDES-BENZ

MERCEDES-BENZ

Typ 190 SL

Drei Wünsche – auf einmal erfüllt

Hohe Leistung, ausgeprägter Komfort und betriebliche Unempfindlichkeit – drei Eigenschaften, deren Verwirklichung in einem Fahrzeug der Wunschtraum eines jeden Automobilisten ist – sind die hervorstechenden Merkmale des neuen Mercedes-Benz Tourensportwagens 190 SL. Als Reisewagen und für tägliche Fahrten im Stadtverkehr bietet der rassig-elegante Roadster für einen Wagen sportlichen Charakters ein ungewöhnlich hohes Maß an Fahrkomfort, Zuverlässigkeit und Wirtschaftlichkeit. Seine zeitsparende Schnelligkeit und Geräumigkeit, seine leichte Bedienung und überragende Sicherheit machen ihn zum vorzüglichen Gebrauchsfahrzeug. Darüber hinaus ermöglichen seine hohe Leistung und imponierenden Fahreigenschaften ein sportliches Fahren. Zur Gewichtsverminderung können die Türen gegen Leichtmetall-Sporttüren mit tiefem Armausschnitt, die Windschutzscheibe gegen ein Plexiglas-Schild ausgetauscht und das Verdeck sowie die Stoßstangen abgenommen werden. Mit dem Aufsetzen des formschönen Leichtmetalldaches wird der 190 SL zum gediegenen, repräsentativen Coupé mit allen Annehmlichkeiten eines großen, komfortablen Tourenwagens. Die technisch glänzende Lösung des Problems, drei so verschiedene Wagenformen in einem Typ zusammenzufassen, liefert einen überzeugenden Beweis für das reife Können seiner Konstrukteure. Bei aller Vielseitigkeit des 190 SL bleibt jedoch der traditionelle Mercedes-Benz-Grundsatz unbedingter Sicherheit voll gewahrt. Sie bildet den umfassenden Rahmen, in dem die Schnelligkeit, der Komfort und die Schönheit dieses neuen Tourenwagens harmonisch vereint sind.

Roadster

Coupé

Sportlicher Roadster

MERCEDES-BENZ Type 190 SL
Three Wishes-fulfilled at once

High performance, luxurious comfort and undemanding operation-three qualities whose realization in one vehicle is the dream of every motorist-are the outstanding characteristics of the new Mercedes-Benz 190 SL touring sports car. For long trips and daily driving in city traffic, the refined, elegant roadster offers an unusually high degree of riding comfort, reliability and economy for a car of sporting character. Its time-saving speed and roominess, its easy maintenance and outstanding safety make it an exemplary utility vehicle. Beyond that, its high performance and impressive handling qualities make sporty driving possible. For weight reduction, the doors can be exchanged for light metal sport doors with deep cutouts, the windshield for a plexiglas shield, and the top and bumpers can be removed. By putting on the beautifully shaped metal roof, the 190 SL becomes a refined, impressive coupe with all the conveniences of a big, comfortable touring car. The technically superb solution of the problem of combining three so different cars in one type offers convincing proof of the mature ability of its constructors. With all the versatility of the 190 SL, the traditional Mercedes-Benz basis of unqualified safety remains fully guaranteed. It provides the inclusive framework in which the speed, comfort and beauty of this new touring car and harmoniously united.

Roadster
Coupe
Sports roadster

Of the three wishes, two were definitely fulfilled: the sports roadster with cutout doors remained a dream . . .

For the not at all so small luggage space of the 190 SL there was a special five-piece set of luggage for optimal space utilization.

16

Kraft und Tempo – leicht beherrscht

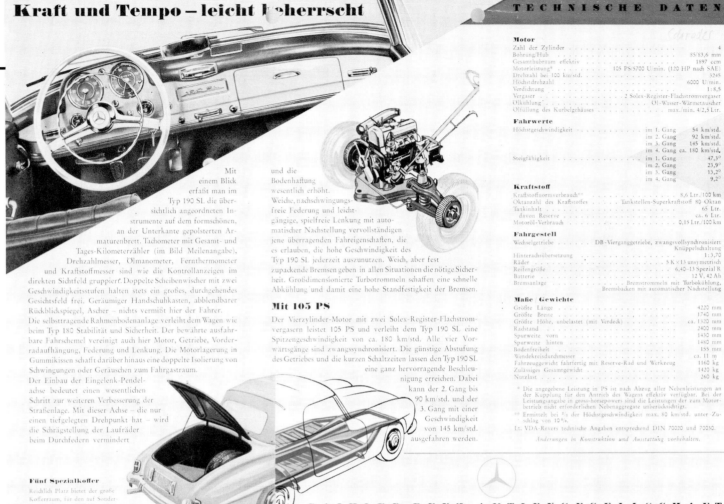

...er and speed-easily controlled

...a glance one can read the Type 190 SL's ...ruments, arranged for easy viewing on the ...utifully formed dashboard, with its upholstered ...om edge. Speedometer with total and daily ...meters(miles shown in the picture), tach-...eter, oil pressure gauge, engine thermometer ...fuel gauge are grouped, as are the control ...cators, in your direct field of vision. Dual ...dshield wipers with two speeds always keep a ...e, unbroken field of vision clear. A roomy ...ve compartment, glare-free rear-view mirror, ...rays-the driver misses nothing here. The self-...ring frame-bottom construction lends the car ...ility and safety, as in the Type 180. The ...ovable subframe unites the motor, gearbox, ...t wheel mountings, suspension and steering ... too. The motor mounted on rubber pads also ...vides doubled insulation of the passenger area ...n vibrations and noises. The construction of ...single-joint swing axle is an important step ...ard further improvement of the roadholding. ...h this axle-which has only one low-lying ...ning point-the angling of the wheels by the ...ings is minimized and the ground clearance is ...siderably raised. Soft springs, suspension ...hout recoil, and light, easy steering with ...omatic return complete the outstanding ...ring characteristics that allow the high speed of ... 190 SL to be used at any time. Soft but firmly ...ding brakes provide the necessary safety in all ...ations. Large-dimensioned turbo drums make ...quick cooling and thus the high durability of ... brakes.

...h 105 HP

...four-cylinder motor with two Solex horizontal ...buretors produces 105 HP and gives the Type ...SL a top speed of about 180 kph. All four ...ward speeds are synchronized. The favorable ...r ratios and quick shifting times allow the ...pe 190 SL to attain truly outstanding ...eleration. In the process, second gear can be ...d up to 90 kph and third gear up to a speed of ... kph.

...e special suitcases

...e large luggage space offers ample room, for ...ich three special suitcases are available ...ionally. Two more suitcases fit into the space ...ind the seats.

...AIMLER-BENZ CORPORATION
...UTTGART-UNTERTURKHEIM

...th top up   The open roadster   For sporting events

...pe 190 SL
...ouring sports car that proves its format everywhere.

Mit
einem Blick
erfaßt man im
Typ 190 SL die über-
sichtlich angeordneten Instrumente auf dem formschönen,
an der Unterkante gepolsterten Armaturenbrett. Tachometer mit Gesamt- und
Tages-Kilometerzähler (im Bild Meilenangabe),
Drehzahlmesser, Ölmanometer, Fernthermometer
und Kraftstoffmesser sind wie die Kontrollanzeigen im
direkten Sichtfeld gruppiert. Doppelte Scheibenwischer mit zwei
Geschwindigkeitsstufen halten stets ein großes, durchgehendes
Gesichtsfeld frei. Geräumiger Handschuhkasten, abblendbarer
Rückblickspiegel, Ascher – nichts vermißt hier der Fahrer.
Die selbsttragende Rahmenbodenanlage verleiht dem Wagen wie
beim Typ 180 Stabilität und Sicherheit. Der bewährte ausfahr-
bare Fahrschemel vereinigt auch hier Motor, Getriebe, Vorderradaufhängung, Federung und Lenkung. Die Motorlagerung in
Gummikissen schafft darüber hinaus eine doppelte Isolierung von
Schwingungen oder Geräuschen zum Fahrgastraum.
Der Einbau der Eingelenk-Pendel-
achse bedeutet einen wesentlichen
Schritt zur weiteren Verbesserung der
Straßenlage. Mit dieser Achse – die nur
einen tiefgelegten Drehpunkt hat – wird
die Schrägstellung der Laufräder
beim Durchfedern vermindert

und die
Bodenhaftung
wesentlich erhöht.
Weiche, nachschwingungs-
freie Federung und leichtgängige, spielfreie Lenkung mit automatischer Nachstellung vervollständigen
jene überragenden Fahreigenschaften, die
es erlauben, die hohe Geschwindigkeit des
Typ 190 SL jederzeit auszunutzen. Weich, aber fest
zupackende Bremsen geben in allen Situationen die nötige Sicherheit. Großdimensionierte Turbotrommeln schaffen eine schnelle
Abkühlung und damit eine hohe Standfestigkeit der Bremsen.

Mit 105 PS

Der Vierzylinder-Motor mit zwei Solex-Register-Flachström-
vergasern leistet 105 PS und verleiht dem Typ 190 SL eine
Spitzengeschwindigkeit von ca. 180 km/std. Alle vier Vorwärtsgänge sind zwangssynchronisiert. Die günstige Abstufung
des Getriebes und die kurzen Schaltzeiten lassen den Typ 190 SL
eine ganz hervorragende Beschleu-
nigung erreichen. Dabei
kann im 2. Gang bis
90 km/std. und im
3. Gang mit einer
Geschwindigkeit
von 145 km/std.
ausgefahren werden.

Fünf Spezialkoffer

Reichlich Platz bietet der große
Kofferraum, für den auf Sonderwunsch drei Spezialkoffer geliefert
werden. Zwei weitere Koffer nimmt
der Raum hinter den Sitzen auf.

Motor

Zahl der Zylinder	4
Bohrung/Hub	85/83,6 mm
Gesamthubraum effektiv	1897 ccm
Motorleistung*	105 PS/5700 U/min. (120 HP nach SAE)
Drehzahl bei 100 km/std.	3245
Höchstdrehzahl	6000 U/min.
Verdichtung	1:8,5
Vergaser	2 Solex-Register-Flachstromvergaser
Ölkühlung	Öl-Wasser-Wärmetauscher
Ölfüllung des Kurbelgehäuses	max./min. 4/2,5 Ltr.

Fahrwerte

Höchstgeschwindigkeit	im 1. Gang	54 km/std.
	im 2. Gang	92 km/std.
	im 3. Gang	145 km/std.
	im 4. Gang ca.	180 km/std.
Steigfähigkeit	im 1. Gang	47,3°
	im 2. Gang	23,9°
	im 3. Gang	13,2°
	im 4. Gang	9,2°

Kraftstoff

Kraftstoffnormverbrauch**	8,6 Ltr./100 km
Oktanzahl des Kraftstoffes	Tankstellen-Superkraftstoff 80 Oktan
Tankinhalt	65 Ltr.
davon Reserve	ca. 6 Ltr.
Motoröl-Verbrauch	0,15 Ltr./100 km

Fahrgestell

Wechselgetriebe	DB-Vierganggetriebe, zwangsvollsynchronisiert Knüppelschaltung
Hinterachsübersetzung	1:3,70
Räder	5 K ×13 unsymmetrisch
Reifengröße	6,40-13 Spezial R
Batterie	12 V, 42 Ah
Bremsanlage	Bremstrommeln mit Turbokühlung, Bremsbacken mit automatischer Nachstellung

Maße Gewichte

Größte Länge	4220 mm
Größte Breite	1740 mm
Größte Höhe, unbelastet (mit Verdeck)	1320 mm
Radstand	2400 mm
Spurweite vorn	1430 mm
Spurweite hinten	1482 mm
Bodenfreiheit	155 mm
Wendekreisdurchmesser	ca. 11 m
Fahrzeuggewicht fahrfertig mit Reserve-Rad und Werkzeug	1160 kg
Zulässiges Gesamtgewicht	1420 kg
Nutzlast	260 kg

* Die angegebene Leistung in PS ist nach Abzug aller Nebenleistungen an der Kupplung für den Antrieb des Wagens effektiv verfügbar. Bei der Leistungsangabe in gross-horsepowers sind die Leistungen der zum Motorbetrieb nicht erforderlichen Nebenaggregate unberücksichtigt.
** Ermittelt bei ⅔ der Höchstgeschwindigkeit max. 80 km/std. mit Zuschlag von 10%.
Lt. VDA-Revers technische Angaben entsprechend DIN 70020 und 70030.

Änderungen in Konstruktion und Ausstattung vorbehalten.

DAIMLER-BENZ AKTIENGESELLSCHAFT
STUTTGART-UNTERTÜRKHEIM

305   Printed in Germany 355 H – 520

Mit geschlossenem Verdeck

Der offene Roadster

Für sportlichen Einsatz

TYP *190 SL*

Ein Tourensportwagen, der sein Format überall beweist

Kurvenfest

Was ungezählte Mercedes-Benz-Besitzer als eine der vollkommensten Eigenschaften ihrer Fahrzeuge kennen und schätzen gelernt haben, ist beim Typ 190 SL.

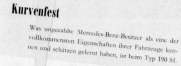

durch den besonders tiefliegenden Schwerpunkt noch mehr ausgeprägt: durch seine überragende Straßenlage fährt man selbst auf schlechten, kurvenreichen Strecken jederzeit ruhig und sicher in zügiger Fahrt. Gerade hier zeigt sich, wie überragend die Bodenhaftung der Vorderräder und die fahrtechnischen Eigenschaften der Eingelenk-Pendelachse sind.

Die Rahmen-Bodenanlage mit Fahrschemel und Eingelenk-Pendelachse.

Wohltemperiert

zu jeder Jahreszeit bleibt der Innenraum dank des sorgfältig durchdachten Heizungs- und Belüftungssystems, das Fahrer und Fahrgast unabhängig voneinander einstellen können. Je zwei Hebel links und rechts am Armaturenbrett erlauben eine feine Dosierung der getrennt zugeführten Luftmenge zur Windschutzscheibe oder zum Fußraum vor beiden Sitzen. In der Mitte des Armaturenbretts liegen die beiden Hebel zur Regulierung der Wärmezufuhr für die linke beziehungsweise rechte Wagenhälfte. Unabhängig von den Launen des Wetters befinden sich die Insassen stets im Klima ihrer Wahl.

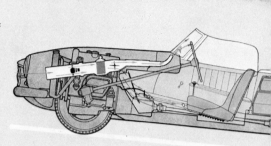

Eingelenk-Pendelachse

Eine technische Besonderheit des Typ 190 SL ist die richtungsweisende Konstruktion der Eingelenk-Pendelachse. Durch nur einen tiefgelegten Drehpunkt werden die Halbachsen der Hinterachse länger und damit der Sturz – die Schrägneigung der Hinterräder – wesentlich geringer, während die Bodenhaftung weitaus verbessert werden konnte.

- großdimensionierte hydraulische Stoßdämpfer
- eigenreibungsfreie Spiralfeder
- gummigelagerter Verbindungshebel zur Rahmen-Bodenanlage

Technik, die i...

Aus Renner... radaufhäng... einzeln mit ... Fahrschem... Großdimensi... auch in Kurve... sichere Boden... aufhängung er... Fahreigenschaf... die hohe Gesc... voll auszunutze...

Roadholding

What countless Mercedes-Benz owners have learned to know and value as one of the most highly developed qualities of their vehicles, is even more pronounced in the 190 SL by the particularly low-lying center of gravity: thanks to its outstanding roadholding, one always rides quietly and safely in smooth motion on even rough and winding roads. Here is where it shows how outstanding the roadholding of the front wheels and the technical quality of the single-joint swing axle.
The frame-bottom unit with front subframe and single-joint swing axle.

Well-Tempered in every season is the interior, thanks to the carefully conceived heating and ventilation system, which the driver and passenger can adjust independently of each other. Two levers each on the left and right sides of the dashboard allow a fine apportioning of the separately conducted air mass to the windshield or the foot space before both seats. In the center of the dashboard are the two levels for regulating the heat to the left and right halves of the car. Independent of the moods of the weather, the occupants always find themselves in the climate of their choice.

Single-Joint Swing Axle

A technical specialty of the Type 190 SL is the ultramodern construction of the single-joint swing axle. With only one low-lying differential, the half-axles of the rear axle are longer, and thus the toe-in-the tendency of the rear wheels to go out of plumb-is considerably less, while the roadholding could be improved considerably.
. large-size hydraulic shock absorbers
. friction-free coil springs
. rubber-mounted joint lever to the frame-bottom

Technology Refined in Racing

The front suspension of the 190 SL is developed from racing experience. The wheels are suspended individually from the subframe by triangular wishbone transverse links.
Large-size hydraulic shock absorbers make for safe roadholding, even on curves and uneven surfaces. Swing axle and front wheel suspension together provide those enchanting driving characteristics that allow the high speed of the Type 190 SL to be utilized fully.

¿page 19¡

Playfully Easy to Steer

The light and play-free Daimler-Benz recirculating ball steering with automatic return give the Type 190 SL driver a soft but safe contact with the road even at high speed. A steering damper prevents the unevenness of the road from being transmitted to the steering wheel.
Large-Size Brakes
Softly but firmly, the large-size hydraulic brakes take hold and provide the necessary security in all situations. With their turbo-drums, they achieve fast cooling and thus high brake durability.

The very stable frame-bottom unit of the 190 SL had been taken from the Type 180 sedan. The front axle and powerplant unit were combined in a so-called subframe that could be detached completely.

Technical Data of the Mercedes-Benz 180

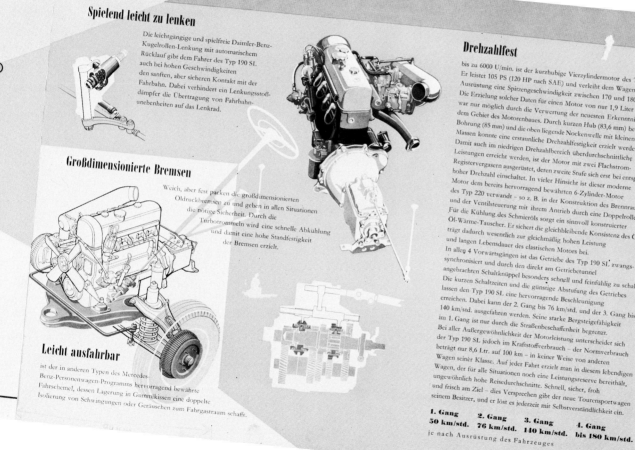

Spielend leicht zu lenken

Die leichtgängige und spielfreie Daimler-Benz-Kugelrollen-Lenkung mit automatischem Rücklauf gibt dem Fahrer des Typ 190 SL auch bei hohen Geschwindigkeiten den sanften, aber sicheren Kontakt mit der Fahrbahn. Dabei verhindert ein Lenkungsstoßdämpfer die Übertragung von Fahrbahnunebenheiten auf das Lenkrad.

Großdimensionierte Bremsen

Weich, aber fest packen die großdimensionierten Öldruckbremsen zu und geben in allen Situationen die nötige Sicherheit. Durch die Turbotrommeln wird eine schnelle Abkühlung und damit eine hohe Standfestigkeit der Bremsen erzielt.

Leicht ausfahrbar

ist der in anderen Typen des Mercedes-Benz-Personenwagen-Programms hervorragend bewährte Fahrschemel, dessen Lagerung in Gummikissen eine doppelte Isolierung von Schwingungen oder Geräuschen zum Fahrgastraum schafft.

Drehzahlfest

bis zu 6000 U/min. ist der kurzhubige Vierzylindermotor des Typ 190 SL. Er leistet 105 PS (120 HP nach SAE) und verleiht dem Wagen je nach Ausrüstung eine Spitzengeschwindigkeit zwischen 170 und 180 km/std. Die Erzielung solcher Daten für einen Motor von nur 1,9 Liter Hubraum war nur möglich durch die Verwertung der neuesten Erkenntnisse auf dem Gebiet des Motorenbaues. Durch kurzen Hub (83,6 mm) bei großer Bohrung (85 mm) und die oben liegende Nockenwelle mit klein bewegten Massen konnte eine erstaunliche Drehzahlfestigkeit erzielt werden. Damit auch im niedrigen Drehzahlbereich überdurchschnittliche Leistungen erreicht werden, ist der Motor mit zwei Flachstrom-Registervergasern ausgerüstet, deren zweite Stufe sich erst bei entsprechend hoher Drehzahl einschaltet. In vieler Hinsicht ist dieser moderne Motor dem bereits hervorragend bewährten 6-Zylinder-Motor des Typ 220 verwandt – so z. B. in der Konstruktion des Brennraumes und der Ventilsteuerung mit ihrem Antrieb durch eine Doppelrollenkette. Für die Kühlung des Schmieröls sorgt ein sinnvoll konstruierter Öl-Wärme-Tauscher. Er sichert die gleichbleibende Konsistenz des Öls und trägt dadurch wesentlich zur gleichmäßig überdurchschnittlichen Leistung und langen Lebensdauer des elastischen Motors bei.

In alleg 4 Vorwärtsgängen ist das Getriebe des Typ 190 SL zwangssynchronisiert und durch den direkt am Getriebetunnel angebrachten Schaltknüppel besonders schnell und feinfühlig zu schalten. Die kurzen Schaltzeiten und die günstige Abstufung des Getriebes lassen den Typ 190 SL eine hervorragende Beschleunigung erreichen. Dabei kann der 2. Gang bis 76 km/std. und der 3. Gang bis 140 km/std. ausgefahren werden. Seine starke Bergsteigefähigkeit im 1. Gang ist nur durch die Straßenbeschaffenheit begrenzt. Bei aller Außergewöhnlichkeit der Motorleistung unterscheidet sich der Typ 190 SL jedoch im Kraftstoffverbrauch – der Normverbrauch beträgt nur 8,6 Ltr. auf 100 km – in keiner Weise von anderen Wagen seiner Klasse. Auf jeder Fahrt erzielt man in diesem lebendigen Wagen, der für alle Situationen noch eine Leistungsreserve bereithält, ungewöhnlich hohe Reisedurchschnitte. Schnell, sicher, froh und frisch am Ziel – dies Versprechen gibt der neue Tourensportwagen seinem Besitzer, und er löst es jederzeit mit Selbstverständlichkeit ein.

1. Gang	2. Gang	3. Gang	4. Gang
50 km/std.	76 km/std.	140 km/std.	bis 180 km/std.

je nach Ausrüstung des Fahrzeuges

Running Safely up to 6000 rpm is the short-stroke four-cylinder motor of the Type 190 SL. It produces 105 HP (120 SAE HP) and gives the car, depending on how it is equipped, as top speed between 170 and 180 kph. The achievement of such figures for a motor of only 1.9-liter displacement was only possible through the evaluation of the most recent knowledge in the field of motor construction. With its short stroke (83.6 mm) and large bore (85 mm) and the overhead camshaft with small moved masses, a remarkable durability could be attained. So that above-average performance could be attained even at low engine speeds, the motor is equipped with two horizontal carburetors whose second stage is activated only at appropriately high engine speeds. In many ways this modern motor is related to the already superbly proven 6-cylinder motor of the Type 220-for example, in the construction of the combustion chamber and valve activation with their power coming through a double-roller chain. A smartly built oil heat exchanger takes care of cooling the lubrication oil. It assures the unchanging consistency of the oil and thus contributes considerably to unchanging high performance and a long lifetime for the flexible motor.

In all four forward speeds, the gears of the Type 190 SL is fully synchronized and can be shifted especially quickly and precisely by the shift lever mounted directly on the drive tunnel. The quick shifting times and the favorable gear ratios allow the Type 190 SL to attain outstanding acceleration. Second gear can be maintained up to 76 kph, and third gear up to 140 kph. Its strong mountain-climbing capability in first gear is limited only by the nature of the road. With all this extraordinary performance of the motor, the Type 190 SL does not differ in any way-the normal consumption is only 8.6 liters per 100 km-from other cars of its class. On every drive in this lively car that still retains a power reserve for all situations, one achieves unusually high average speeds. Fast, safe, happy and fresh at the end-this promise is given to its owner by this new touring sports car, and naturally it keeps its promise every time.

1st gear
2nd gear
3rd gear 4th gear
50 kph
76 kph
140 kph
to 180 kph

depending on the vehicle's equipment

Only Minor Changes

Serienmäßig eingebaute Neuerungen:

ATE-Bremsgerät, Lichthupe, Entfroster- und Heizgebläse, Starktonhorn, Handschuhkasten-Schloß

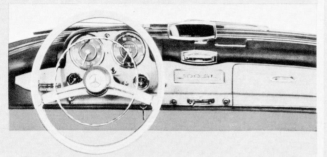

Sicheren Halt

und Bequemlichkeit bei jeder Fahrweise geben die Sitze, die in Längsrichtung leicht zu verstellen sind. Sie sind mit den Farben der übrigen Innenausstattung und der Karosserie zu reizvoller Harmonie abgestimmt. Bei jeder Wagenausführung läßt sich gegen Mehrpreis im Fond ein dritter Sitz quer zur Fahrtrichtung anbringen.

Kraft und Tempo — leicht beherrscht

Mit einem Blick erfaßt man im 190 SL die übersichtlich angeordneten Instrumente auf dem formschönen, an der Ober- und Unterkante mit Texleder bezogenen Armaturenbrett. Tachometer mit Gesamt- und Tageskilometerzähler, Drehzahlmesser, Ölmanometer, Kühlwasser-Fernthermometer und Kraftstoffmesser sind gleich den Kontrollanzeigen im direkten Blickwinkel gruppiert. Ein Scheibenwischerpaar mit zwei Geschwindigkeitsstufen hält stets ein großes, durchgehendes Sichtfeld frei.

Die selbsttragende Rahmenbodenanlage verleiht dem 190 SL Festigkeit und Verwindungssteifheit. Motor, Getriebe, Vorderradaufhängung und Lenkung sind in dem nach vorne ausfahrbaren Fahrschemel vereint. Darüber hinaus schafft die Motorlagerung in Gummikissen eine doppelte Isolierung von Schwingungen und Geräuschen zum Fahrgastraum. Die Eingelenk-Pendelachse hinten trägt wesentlich zu der überragenden

Straßenhaftung des 190 SL bei, indem sie die Führung der Hinterräder auch bei schärfster Fahrweise sichert.

Die weiche, nachschwingungsfreie Federung und die leichtgängige Lenkung vervollständigen das Gesamtbild der hervorstechenden Fahreigenschaften dieses schnellen Wagens. Weich, aber fest packen die großdimensionierten Turbobremsen zu und geben auch bei starker Beanspruchung durch ihre große Standfestigkeit stets die nötige Sicherheit.

105 PS leistet der elastische Vierzylinder-Motor bei völlig ausgeglichenem Lauf. Er verleiht dem 190 SL je nach Ausrüstung eine Spitzengeschwindigkeit von ca. 170 bis 180 km/std. Die günstige Abstufung des Getriebes und die kurzen Schaltzeiten geben diesem sportlichen Wagen eine ganz hervorragende Beschleunigung und Steigfähigkeit. Dabei kann der 2. Gang bis zu 76 km/std. und der 3. Gang bis zu einer Geschwindigkeit von ca. 120 km/std. ausgefahren werden.

TECHNISCHE DATEN

Motor

Zahl der Zylinder	4
Bohrung/Hub	85/83,6 mm
Gesamthubraum effektiv	1897 ccm
Motorleistung*	105 PS/5700 U/min. (120 HP nach SAE)
Drehzahl bei 100 km/std.	3370 U/min.
Höchstdrehzahl	6000 U/min.
Verdichtung	8,5 : 1
Vergaser	2 Solex-Register-Flachstromvergaser
Ölkühlung	Öl-Wasser-Wärmetauscher
Ölfüllung des Kurbelgehäuses	max./min. 4/2,5 Ltr.

Fahrwerte

Höchstgeschwindigkeit (je nach Aufbau)	im 1. Gang	50 km/std.
	im 2. Gang	76 km/std.
	im 3. Gang	ca. 120 km/std.
	im 4. Gang ca.	170–180 km/std.
Steigfähigkeit	im 1. Gang	ca. 50 %
	im 2. Gang	ca. 30 %
	im 3. Gang	ca. 17 %
	im 4. Gang	ca. 9,5 %

Kraftstoff

Kraftstoffnormverbrauch**	8,6 Ltr./100 km
Oktanzahl des Kraftstoffes	Tankstellen-Super- bzw. Benzin-Benzol-Kraftstoff mit mind. 89 Oktan nach Research-Methode (ROZ)
Tankinhalt	65 Ltr.
davon Reserve	ca. 6 Ltr.
Motoröl-Verbrauch	0,15 Ltr./100 km

Fahrgestell

Wechselgetriebe	DB-Vierganggetriebe, zwangsvollsynchronisiert Knüppelschaltung
Hinterachsübersetzung	1 : 3,9
Räder	5 K × 13 unsymmetrisch
Reifengröße	6,40–13 Spezial RS
Batterie	12 V, 56 Ah
Bremsanlage	Bremstrommeln mit Turbokühlung, Bremsbacken mit automatischer Nachstellung

Maße / Gewichte

Größte Länge	4220 mm
Größte Breite	1740 mm
Größte Höhe, unbelastet (mit Verdeck)	ca. 1320 mm
Radstand	2400 mm
Spurweite vorn	1430 mm
Spurweite hinten	1470 mm
Bodenfreiheit	155 mm
Wendekreisdurchmesser	ca. 11 m
Fahrzeuggewicht fahrfertig mit Reserve-Rad und Werkzeug	1140 kg
Zulässiges Gesamtgewicht	1400 kg
Nutzlast	260 kg

* Die angegebene Leistung in PS ist nach Abzug aller Nebenleistungen an der Kupplung für den Antrieb des Wagens effektiv verfügbar. Bei der Leistungsangabe in gross-horsepowers sind die Leistungen der zum Motorbetrieb nicht erforderlichen Nebenaggregate unberücksichtigt.

** Ermittelt bei ⅔ der Höchstgeschwindigkeit (max. 80 km/std.) unter Zuschlag von 10 %.

Lt. VDA-Revers technische Angaben entsprechend DIN 70020 und 70030

Änderungen in Konstruktion und Ausstattung vorbehalten.

New standard features

ATE Power Brakes, Flasher, Defroster and Heater Blower, S Horn, Glove Compartment Lock

Safe support and comfort in every kind of driving are prov seats, which are easy to adjust longitudinally. They ar charming harmony with the colors of the other interior f and the body. In every version of the car, a third seat that can transverse position is available for an extra charge.

Power and Speed-Easily Controlled

At a glance one can read the instruments of the Type 190 SL to be seen easily on the dashboard whose upper and lowe covered with leatherette. The speedometer with total odometers, tachometer, oil pressure gauge, water thermo fuel gauge, like the control indicators, are grouped in one's of vision. A pair of windshield wipers with two speeds alw large, unbroken viewing area clear.

The self-bearing frame-bottom chassis unit gives the 190 S and stiffness. Motor, gearbox, front suspension and steering in the subframe that can be detached at the front. In ad motor is mounted in rubber, providing double insulat interior from vibration and noise. The single-joint s contributes significantly to the outstanding roadholding SL, by securing the movement of the rear wheels under hardest driving.

The soft, recoil-free springs and the light steering complete of the outstanding characteristics of this fast car. Softly an large-size turbo brakes hold on and always provide the safety, even under great pressure.

105 HP with completely even running, produced by the fle cylinder motor, give the 190 SL, depending on its equipm speed of approximately 170 to 180 kph. The favorable gear the brief shifting time give this sporty car truly o acceleration and climbing ability. Second gear can be main to 76 kph and third gear up to a speed of about 120 kph.

Ihr guter Stern auf allen Straßen

DAIMLER-BENZ AKTIENGESELLSCHAFT STUTTGART-UNTERTÜRKHEIM

Printed in Germany 316/2

Roadster –
für sportliches
Fahren
und erholsames
Reisen

Roadster-for sporty driving and relaxing travel

Daimler-Benz went to a lot of trouble to give the 190 SL a certain similarity to the 300 SL. They succeeded particularly well in the front aspect.

Thoroughbred temperament

The transmission of the Type 190 SL is fully synchronized in all four forward speeds and can be shifted sportingly fast and easily with the stick shift mounted directly on the transmission tunnel. Its excellent gear ratios let this lively car attain fast acceleration. The second gear can be maintained up to about 76 kph, third gear to about 120 kph. No climb can overpower the powerful motor. You will take extraordinarily high travel speeds for granted as they shorten your quick trips pleasantly.

The motor was based on the six-cylinder type introduced in 1951. The overhead-cam four-cylinder did, though, have a shorter stroke. Two Solex double carburetors provided for fuel preparation.

23

Rassiges Temperament

Thoroughbred Temperament

The transmission of the Type 190 SL is fully synchronized in all four forward speeds and can be shifted sportingly fast and easily with the stick shift mounted directly on the transmission tunnel. Its excellent gear ratios let this lively car attain fast acceleration. The second gear can be maintained up to about 76 kph, third gear to about 120 kph. No climb can overpower the powerful motor. You will take extraordinarily high travel speeds for granted as they shorten your quick trips pleasntly.

Das Getriebe des Typ 190 SL ist in allen vier Vorwärtsgängen zwangssynchronisiert und durch den direkt am Getriebetunnel angebrachten Schalthebel sportlich-schnell und leicht zu schalten. Seine ausgezeichnete Abstufung läßt diesen temperamentvollen Wagen die hohe Beschleunigung erreichen. Dabei kann der 2. Gang bis ca. 76 km/std, der 3. Gang bis ca. 120 km/std ausgefahren werden. Keine Steigung kann den kraftvollen Motor überfordern. Außergewöhnlich hohe Reisedurchschnitte werden Ihnen so zu einer Selbstverständlichkeit, die Ihre eiligen Fahrten angenehm verkürzt.

The motor was based on the six-cylinder type introduced in 1951. The overhead-cam four-cylinder did, though, have a shorter stroke. Two Solex double carburetors provided for fuel preparation.

Performance and Beauty

Wettersorgen kennt man im Typ 190 SL nicht, denn Fahrer und Begleiter können unabhängig voneinander für ihren Platz das Klima schaffen, das ihnen am meisten behagt. Vom Sitz aus können sie die Frischluftzufuhr in Temperatur, Menge und Verteilung zum Fußraum und gegen die Windschutzscheibe fein regulieren. Im Stand oder bei langsamer Fahrt sorgt das serienmäßige Entfrostergebläse für schnelle, angenehme Heizung des Innenraums.

Kraft und Tempo leicht beherrscht

Weather problems are unknown in the Type 190 SL, for driver and passenger can create the most pleasant climate for their space independently of each other. From their seats they can finely regulate the fresh air supply as to temperature, quantity and diversion to the foot space and the windshield. Whether the car is standing still or moving slowly, the standard defroster blower makes for quick, pleasant heating of the interior.

Power and speed, easily controlled

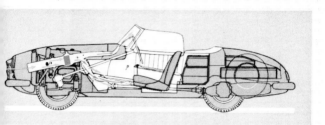

Mit Ihrem Typ 190 SL sind Sie vom ersten Kilometer an vertraut; Sie beherrschen ihn mühelos bei jeder Geschwindigkeit. Tachometer mit Tageskilometerzähler, Drehzahlmesser, Kühlwasserthermometer und Öldruckmesser sind mit einem Blick zu erfassen und sämtliche Bedienungsorgane spielend leicht zu betätigen. Kurz, alles, was das Fahren erfordert und erleichtert – und dazu gehört auch die Lichthupe –, ist sicht- und griffnahe vor Ihnen angeordnet. Als akkustisches Warnsignal entspricht das Starktonhorn dem sportlichen Charakter des Wagens. Auch die Dinge, die Ihrer Bequemlichkeit dienen, sitzen am richtigen Ort – Leselampe, Zigarrenanzünder, Aschenbecher, der abblendbare Rückspiegel, Heizung und Lüftung sowie die Zeituhr auf dem Deckel des großen verschließbaren Handschuhkastens. Das Ergebnis: Sie fühlen sich auch bei scharfer Fahrweise stets behaglich sicher, weil die Schnelligkeit des Wagens weder auf Kosten seines Komforts noch Ihrer Sicherheit geht.

Reisen Sie mit viel Gepäck? Im breiten, tiefen Heck hat es ausreichend Platz, und hinter den Sitzen ist außerdem noch weiterer Raum. Spezialkoffersätze für Heck und Innenraum erhalten Sie auf Sonderwunsch.

With your Type 190 SL you are at home from the first kilometer on; you control it effortlessly at any speed. Speedometer and daily odometer, tachometer, water temperature and oil pressure gauges can be seen at a glance, and all the controls are playfully easy to use. In short, everything that driving requires and that makes driving easier-including the light flashers-is arranged in front of you, easy to see and use. The strong-tone horn is an acoustic warning signal that fits the sporting character of the car. The things that serve your comfort are also located at the right place-reading lamp, cigarette lighter, ashtray, the glare-free rear-view mirror, heating and ventilation, as well as the clock on the lid of the large, locking glove compartment. The result: You always feel comfortably safe, even in hard driving, because the speed of the car does not detract from either its comfort or your safety. Do you travel with a lot of luggage? In the wide, deep trunk it has enough space, and behind the seats there is extra room. Special sets of luggage for trunk and interior space are optionally available.

The 190 SL was not at all a bone-shaking roadster. It was a comfortable car with sufficient space-and thus a popular car for the ladies.

A Car After Your Own Heart . . .

tofahren auch heute nicht nur Mittel zum Zweck, sondern echte Freude, sportlicher Ge-
romantisches Vergnügen sein kann – im Typ 190 SL Roadster wird es gegenwärtig.
m Wagen werden Sie mit Ihrem ganzen Herzen hängen, wenn Sie einmal seine Vorzüge
Gefühl der Überlegenheit ausgekostet haben, die seine bestechende Straßenlage bei jeder
ndigkeit verleiht. Oder Sie genießen Ihre Reise als einen erholsamen Streifzug durch die
it Licht, Luft und Sonne als willkommenen Begleitern. Weite Entfernungen stören Sie
nn der Komfort dieses schnellen Wagens macht Ihnen jeden Kilometer zur Freude. Das
ufklappbare Verdeck schützt Sie vor unliebsamen Überraschungen bei plötzlichem Wet-
el. Die bequemen Sitze geben auch bei scharfer Kurvenfahrt festen Halt. Für Fahrten zu
n der Fond auf Sonderwunsch mit einem schnell montierten Behelfssitz quer zur Fahrt-
ausgestattet werden. Neuerdings wird, wie das Coupé, auch der Roadster mit Chrom-
n oben und unten an den Türen und auf den Schmutzabweisern sowie mit einem Stein-
utz ausgestattet.

e dann abends auf den Boulevards der großen Städte mit Ihrem eleganten Roadster »pro-
a«, sagen es Ihnen die bewundernden Blicke: Sie haben mit Geschmack und Wissen gewählt.

That driving a car today can be not just a means to an end but genuine
joy, sporting enjoyment and romantic pleasure-becomes reality in the
Type 190 SL Roadster. You will get attached to this car with all your
heart once you have sampled its advantages and the feeling of
superiority that its incredible roadholding offers at any speed. Or you
enjoy your trip as a relaxing ride through the world of nature, with
light, air and sun as welcome companions. Long distances do not
disturb you, for the comfort of this fast car makes every kilometer a joy
for you. The quickly raising top protects you from unpleasant
surprises in sudden changes of the weather. The comfortable seats give
firm support even on fast corners. For a trip for three, a quickly
installed auxiliary seat crossways of the car can be added optionally.
And now, like the coupe, the roadster can also be equipped with
chrome decorative stripsat the top and bottom of the doors and the
edges of the dirt deflectors.
And when you "promenade" on the boulevards of the great cities with
your elegant roadster, the admiring glances tell you: you have chosen
with taste and wisdom.

27

Sicherheit von Grund auf

Zur überragenden Straßenlage gesellt sich eine behende Wendigkeit, durch die Sie den dichtesten Verkehr gelassen meistern. Die besonders leichtgängige Daimler-Benz-Kugelumlauflenkung mit automatischer Nachstellung und Lenkungsstoßdämpfer arbeitet äußerst spurgenau mit sanftem, aber sehr sicherem Kontakt zur Fahrbahn.

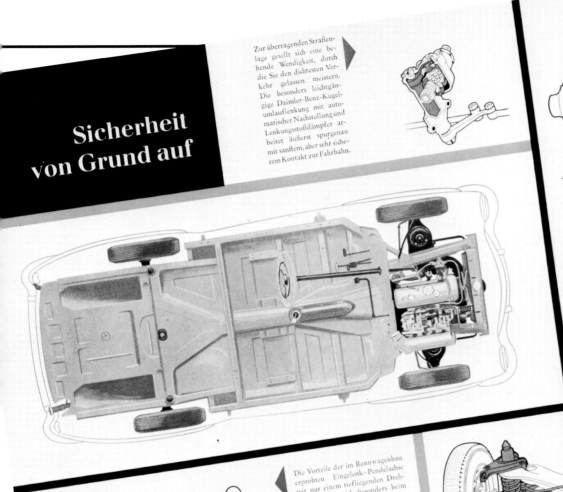

Der Fahrschemel umfaßt den Motor, das Getriebe und die Vorderräder mit Drehstab-Stabilisator, Bremsen und Lenkung als kompakte Einheit. Diese Konstruktion und ihre elastische Lagerung in Gummipolstern an der Rahmenboden-Anlage hat bedeutende Vorteile: sie bewirkt eine präzise Führung und Spurhaltung der Vorderräder – wobei der Drehstab-Stabilisator alle seitlichen Belastungen ausgleicht – und unterbindet obendrein weitgehend die Übertragung von Schwingungen und Fahrgeräuschen zum Innenraum. Da der Fahrschemel sich bequem als Ganzes ausfahren und wieder einbauen läßt, können alle Pflegearbeiten daran leicht, schnell und damit kostensparend durchgeführt werden.

Much emphasis was placed on a pleasant suspension setting. The Mercedes-Benz 190 SL was a car for riding-not a car for racing! Again and again, it was portrayed in advertisements as a touring car.

Die Vorteile der im Rennwagenbau erprobten Eingelenk-Pendelachse mit nur einem tiefliegenden Drehpunkt zeigen sich besonders beim Fahren auf schlechten, kurvenreichen Straßen. Sanft und ohne Stoßen gleitet der Typ 190 SL über alle Bodenunebenheiten weg und zieht wie auf Schienen durch engste Kurven.

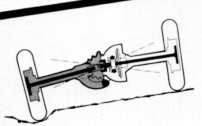

Auch bei der Entwicklung der Vorderradaufhängung standen wertvolle Rennerfahrungen Pate. Die Räder sind einzeln mit Dreiecks-Trapez-Querlenkern am Fahrschemel aufgehängt. Sie erzielen durch die großdimensionierten hydraulischen Stoßdämpfer eine konstant sichere Bodenhaftung und eine besonders elastische Abfederung aller Fahrbahnstöße.

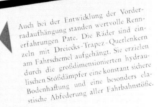

Safety from the ground up

Along with outstanding roadholding goes a nimble agility with which you can master the heaviest traffic calmly. The particularly light Daimler-Benz recirculating-ball steering with automatic return and steering damper works very precisely, with a gentle but very safe contact to the pavement.
The subframe includes the motor, gearbox and front axle with torsion bar stabilizer, brakes and steering as a compact unit. This construction and its elastic mounting on the frame-bottom chassis with rubber pads has noteworthy advantages: it provides a precise direction and

roadholding for the front wheels-whereby the torsion-bar s equalizes all lateral pressures-and also works effectively to m the transmission of vibrations and road noise to the interior. S subframe can be removed easily as a unit and replaced again, an work on it can be done easily, quickly and thus economicall The advantages of the single-joint swing axle with just one lo turning point, proved in racing car construction, are particularly in driving on rough or winding roads. Ger without jolting, the Type 190 SL glides over all uneven surf drives through the sharpest curves as if on rails.
In the development of the front wheel suspension too, valuabl experience has been of assistance. The wheels are attache subframe independently by triangular wishbone transvers With the large-size hydraulic shock absorbers, they achieve a co safe roadholding and a particularly elastic absorption of all the in the road.

28

Coupé -
die individuelle
Form
zu repräsentieren

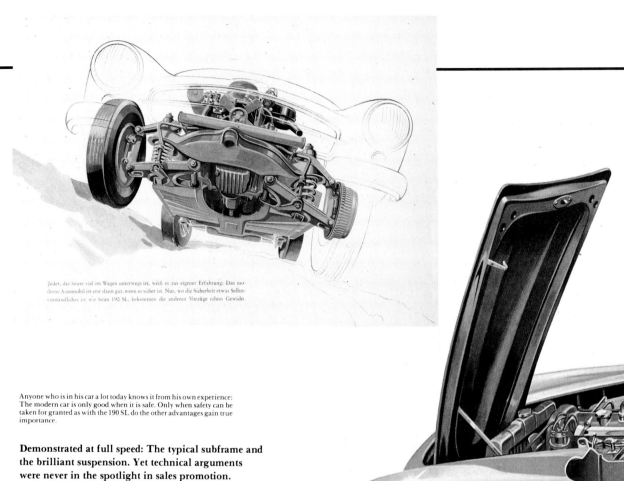

Jeder, der heute viel im Wagen unterwegs ist, weiß es aus eigener Erfahrung: Das moderne Automobil ist erst dann gut, wenn es sicher ist. Nur, wo die Sicherheit etwas Selbstverständliches ist wie beim 190 SL, bekommen die anderen Vorzüge echtes Gewicht.

Anyone who is in his car a lot today knows it from his own experience: The modern car is only good when it is safe. Only when safety can be taken for granted as with the 190 SL do the other advantages gain true importance.

Demonstrated at full speed: The typical subframe and the brilliant suspension. Yet technical arguments were never in the spotlight in sales promotion.

The car at right has the comfortable upholstered seats with which the hardtop model was produced. At extra charge, the hardtop equipment (the roof was always removable) was enhanced with a cloth top.

30

Nicht nur die reiche Ausstattung des 190 SL würde einem großen Reisewagen alle Ehre machen, auch die für einen Tourensportwagen ungewöhnliche Raumfülle vermutet man bei diesem schnittigen und langgestreckten Fahrzeug kaum. Im 190 SL können Sie zu jeder Fahrt ohne Platzsorgen starten, denn der Kofferraum und der große Raum hinter den Vordersitzen nehmen eine Menge Gepäck auf. Sie packen einfach ein, was Sie brauchen und müssen sich nicht mehr mit der Auswahl dringend benötigter Dinge plagen. Der Längsschnitt durch den 190 SL zeigt Ihnen aber noch mehr: Sie sehen hier einmal deutlich den äußerst stabilen Aufbau der Karosserie. Das ist eben Sindelfinger Qualität! Man hat sich bei Mercedes-Benz nicht allein damit begnügt, für ein sportliches Fahrzeug ein reizvolles Kleid zu entwerfen, sondern man war bestrebt, das Optimum an Schönheit, Zweckmäßigkeit und höchster Sicherheit zu erzielen. Das Ergebnis dieser Bemühungen ist einer der elegantesten und sichersten Tourensportwagen, die die Welt heute kennt: der 190 SL.

Not only would the rich furnishings of the 190 SL do honor to a large touring car, but also the spaciousness, unusual for a touring sports car, is hardly expected in this tastefully streamlined vehicle. In the 190 SL you can start any trip without worries about space, for the trunk and the extensive space behind the front seats will hold a lot of luggage. You simply pack in what you need and no longer have to plague yourself with choosing among urgently needed articles. But this cutaway view of the 190 SL shows you more: Here you see clearly the extremely stable construction of the body. That is simply Sindelfingen quality! At Mercedes-Benz they have not been satisfied just to design a charming dress for a sporting vehicle, but tried to aim at the optimum of beauty, practicality and greatest safety. The result of these labors is one of the most elegant and safest touring sports cars that the world knows today: the 190 SL.

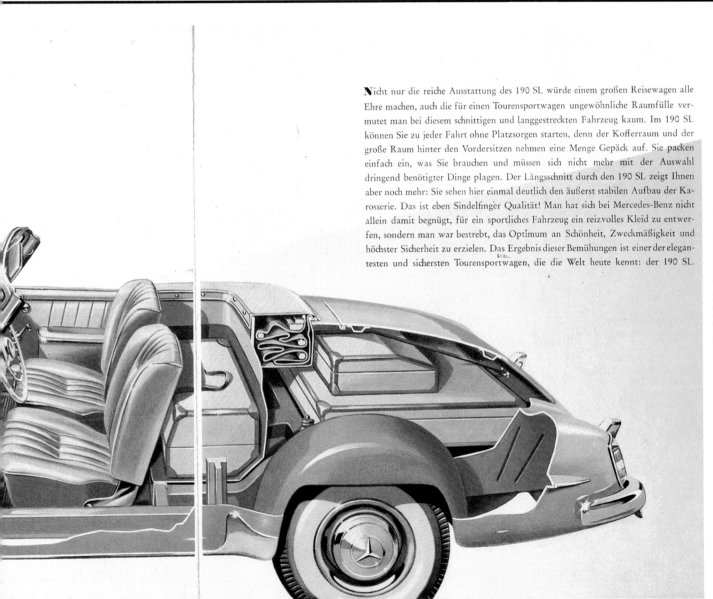

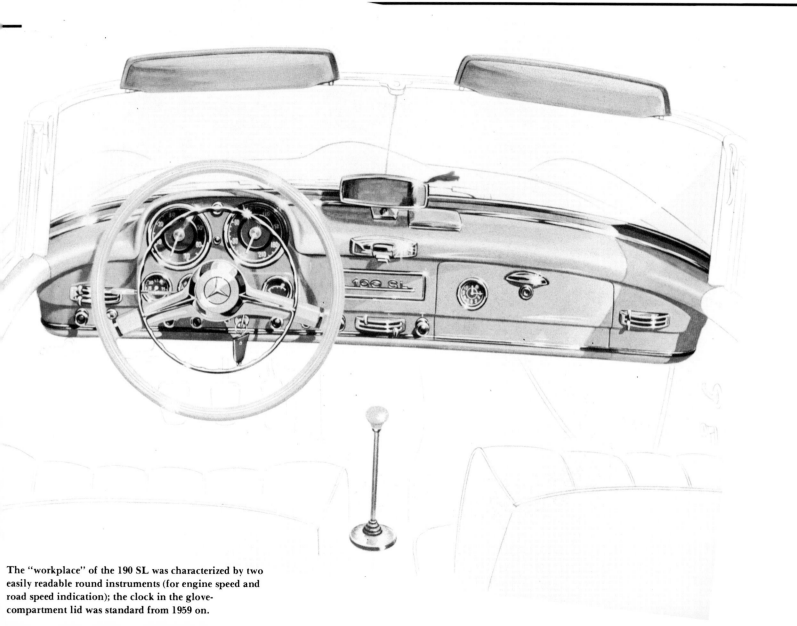

The "workplace" of the 190 SL was characterized by two
easily readable round instruments (for engine speed and
road speed indication); the clock in the glove-
compartment lid was standard from 1959 on.

Hier stellt sich Ihnen der 190 SL als Coupé vor. In dieser repräsentativen Form, sozusagen in seinem Festtagsgewand, hat das rassige Fahrzeug nichts von seinem Temperament verloren – und an Eleganz noch gewonnen. Wo immer Sie auch erscheinen, erregen Sie mit dem bildschönen Wagen Aufsehen – ob Sie nun geschäftlich oder privat unterwegs sind, ob Sie bei Kunden oder bei Ihren Freunden vorfahren. Und die Anerkennung, die man Ihrem 190 SL-Coupé zollt, gilt auch Ihrem sicheren Geschmack. Aber nicht nur die Ästhetik seiner Linien, auch die reichhaltige Innenausstattung betont beim Coupé den repräsentativen Charakter: Polsterbezüge aus echtem, sorgfältig ausgewähltem Leder geben dem Fahrgastraum eine gepflegte Atmosphäre. Die vielen Vorzüge des 190 SL – seine traumhaft sichere Straßenlage, der reich ausgestattete Innenraum, sein Finish bis ins letzte Detail – finden im Coupé ihre Krönung durch die distinguierte äußere Erscheinung. Zu einem solchen Wagen wird man Sie überall beglückwünschen.

Abnehmbares Coupédach

Überall, wo das Dach des Coupés auf der Karosserie aufsitzt, ist durch starke Gummipr[...] für eine staubsichere Abdichtung gesorgt.

Nach Lösen der Knebelgriffe oberhalb der W[...] schutzscheibe und der Verschraubung im H[...] teil ist das Coupédach ohne Aufwand abzuhe[...]

Aus dem repräsentativen Coupé wird so [...] eleganter Roadster, dessen voll versenkb[...] Verdeck (auf Sonderwunsch) Sie nach einfa[...] Montage leicht öffnen und schließen kön[...]

Here the 190 SL introduces itself to you as a coupe. In this impressive form, in its festive attire, so to speak, the thoroughbred car has lost nothing of its temperament-and even gained in elegance. Wherever you appear, you will win admiration with your picture-pretty car-whether you are traveling on business or privately, whether you are seen by customers or friends. And the recognition that one grants to your 190 SL Coupe also applies to your sure taste. Not only the esthetics of its lines, but also the richness of its interior decor stresses the impressive character of the coupe: upholstery covered in carefully selected genuine leather gives the interior a cultivated atmosphere. The many advantages of the 190 SL-its dreamily safe roadholding, the richly appointed interior, its finish to the last detail-find their fulfillment in the coupe along with the distinguished external appearance. One will admire you and such a car everywhere you go.

Removable coupe roof

Wherever the roof of the coupe rests on the bodywork, strong rubber linings provide for dust-free sealing.
After loosening the toggles above the windshield and the screws at the rear, you can lift off the coupe roof with no trouble.
Thus the impressive coupe becomes a roadster whose fully lowering top (available optionally) you can open and close easily after a simple job of mounting it.

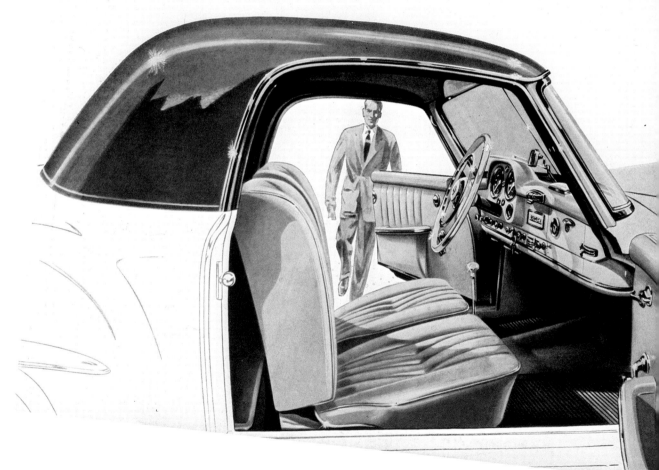

Previous double page: the 190 SL Coupe in all its glory, portrayed in a Mercedes-Benz catalog of 1960.

Above: The interior looks very inviting here. The small auxiliary seat in the back was available as an extra.

Steigen Sie doch einmal ein in den 190 SL. Es fällt schwer, zu entscheiden, was mehr beeindruckt: die bis ins kleinste durchdachte und gestaltete Inneneinrichtung oder die saubere und gediegene Verarbeitung des Materials. Der großzügige Komfort steht dem eines schweren Tourenwagens in nichts nach. Welch ein Unterschied zwischen den spartanisch ausgerüsteten sportlichen Wagen der zwanziger Jahre und der Ausstattung eines 190 SL! Wie nach Maß sind die (beim Roadster mit MB-Tex bezogenen) weichgepolsterten Sitze gearbeitet, die auch bei scharfer Fahrt festen Halt geben. Mühelos sind sie auch während der Fahrt in Längsrichtung zu verstellen; die Lehnen lassen sich außerdem in drei Schräglagen arretieren. Auf den als Armlehnen und als Türziehgriffe ausgearbeiteten, gepolsterten Türtaschen ruhen Ihre Arme bequem. Und alles hat seinen richtigen Platz – Ascher, Zigarrenanzünder, Kartenleselampe, die Bedienungshebel für Lüftung und Heizung, Fensterkurbeln, Türgriffe – alles ist in handlicher Nähe angeordnet. In diesem Wagen reisen Sie stets mit der Freude an den großen und kleinen Annehmlichkeiten des Autofahrens.

Türtaschen und Behelfssitz im Fond

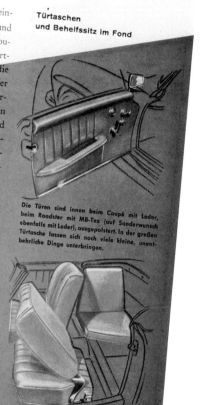

Die Türen sind innen beim Coupé mit Leder, beim Roadster mit MB-Tex (auf Sonderwunsch ebenfalls mit Leder), ausgepolstert. In der großen Türtasche lassen sich noch viele kleine, unentbehrliche Dinge unterbringen.

Für Fahrten mit drei Personen kann der Fond auf Sonderwunsch auch mit einem quer zur Fahrtrichtung eingebauten Behelfssitz ausgestattet werden. Er ist schnell ein- oder ausgebaut.

Go ahead and get into the 190 SL. It is hard to decide what is more impressive: the interior decor, planned and built to the last detail, or the neat and tasteful use of the materials. The lavish comfort is in no way inferior to that of a large sedan. What a difference between the Spartan furnishings of sports cars in the Twenties and the furnishings of a 190 SL! The soft upholstered seats (covered with MB-Tex leatherette in the Roadster) are made as if to your measurements, and they hold you firmly even on sharp curves. They can also be adjusted longitudinally with ease, even while underway; the tilt of the backs can also be adjusted. Your arms rest comfortably on the upholstered door pockets, which are made to serve as armrests and door-closing grips. And everything is in its proper place-ashtray, cigarette lighter, map-reading lamp, the control levers for ventilation and heating, window cranks, door handles-everything is close and handy. You can always ride in this car with the pleasures of the great and small amenities of auto travel.

Door pockets and auxiliary rear seat.
The interiors of the Coupe doors are covered in leather, those of the Roadster in MB-Tex leatherette (optionally also with leather). Many small necessary articles can be carried in the big door pockets.
For trips with three people, the rear can optionally be equipped with an auxiliary seat, mounted transversely. It can be installed and removed quickly.

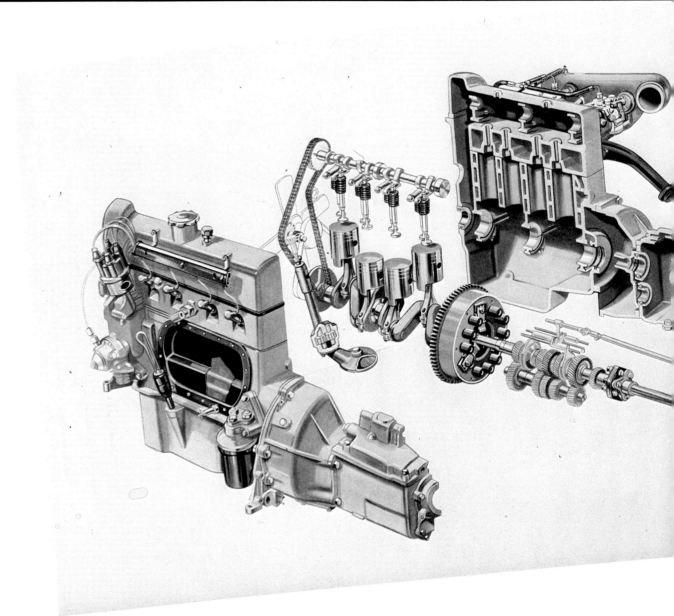

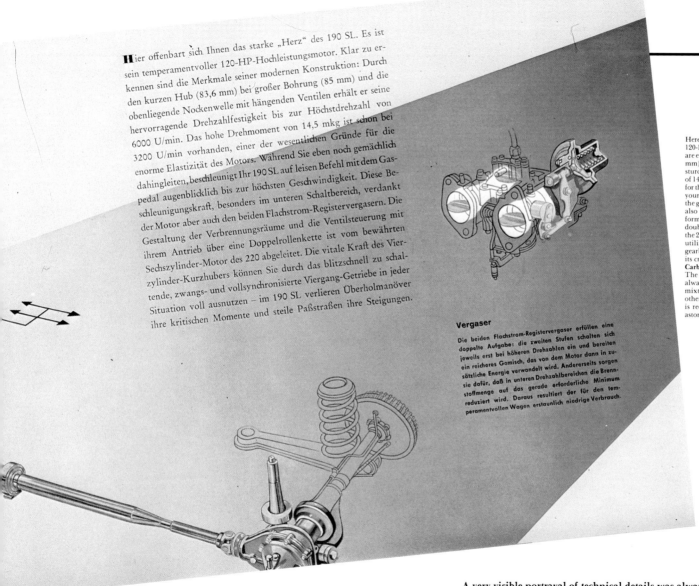

Hier offenbart sich Ihnen das starke „Herz" des 190 SL. Es ist sein temperamentvoller 120-HP-Hochleistungsmotor. Klar zu erkennen sind die Merkmale seiner modernen Konstruktion: Durch den kurzen Hub (83,6 mm) bei großer Bohrung (85 mm) und die obenliegende Nockenwelle mit hängenden Ventilen erhält er seine hervorragende Drehzahlfestigkeit bis zur Höchstdrehzahl von 6000 U/min. Das hohe Drehmoment von 14,5 mkg ist schon bei 3200 U/min vorhanden, einer der wesentlichen Gründe für die enorme Elastizität des Motors. Während Sie eben noch gemächlich dahingleiten, beschleunigt Ihr 190 SL auf leisen Befehl mit dem Gaspedal augenblicklich bis zur höchsten Geschwindigkeit. Diese Beschleunigungskraft, besonders im unteren Schaltbereich, verdankt der Motor aber auch den beiden Flachstrom-Registervergasern. Die Gestaltung der Verbrennungsräume und die Ventilsteuerung mit ihrem Antrieb über eine Doppelrollenkette ist vom bewährten Sechszylinder-Motor des 220 abgeleitet. Die vitale Kraft des Vierzylinder-Kurzhubers können Sie durch das blitzschnell zu schaltende, zwangs- und vollsynchronisierte Viergang-Getriebe in jeder Situation voll ausnutzen — im 190 SL verlieren Überholmanöver ihre kritischen Momente und steile Paßstraßen ihre Steigungen.

Vergaser

Die beiden Flachstrom-Registervergaser erfüllen eine doppelte Aufgabe: die zweiten Stufen schalten sich jeweils erst bei höheren Drehzahlen ein und bereiten ein reicheres Gemisch, das von dem Motor dann in zusätzliche Energie verwandelt wird. Andererseits sorgen sie dafür, daß in unteren Drehzahlbereichen die Brennstoffmenge auf das gerade erforderliche Minimum reduziert wird. Daraus resultiert der für den temperamentvollen Wagen erstaunlich niedrige Verbrauch.

Here the strong "heart" of the 190 SL is exposed to you. It is its spirited 120-HP high-performance motor. The signs of its modern construction are easy to recognize: With its short stroke (83.6 mm) and wide bore (85 mm) and its overhead camshaft with dropped valves, it is outstandingly sturdy all the way up to its highest speed of 6000 rpm. The high torque of 14.5 mkg is already at hand at 3200 rpm, one of the essential reasons for the motor's enormous flexibility. While you glide along pleasantly, your 190 SL accelerates instantly to its highest speed at a mere touch of the gas pedal. This accelerating power, especially in the lower gears, is also made possible by the motor's two horizontal carburetors. The form of the combustion chambers and the valve activation, driven by a double roller chain, are derived from the proven six-cylinder motor of the 220. The vital power of the short-stroke four-cylinder engine can be utilized fully in any situation via the fully synchronized four-speed gearbox that can be shifted lightning-fast in the 190 SL, passing loses its critical moments and steep roads lose their steepness.

Carburetors

The two horizontal carburetors fulfill a pair of tasks: the second stages always switch on only at high engine speeds and prepare a richer mixture, which is then turned to extra energy by the motor. On the other hand, they make sure that at low engine speeds the fuel mixture is reduced to the minimum required at the time. The result is the astonishingly low fuel consumption of the lively motor.

A very visible portrayal of technical details was always the custom at Daimler-Benz. In this picture of the motor, one can clearly recognize the overhead camshaft, driven by a roller chain.

Hinter seinem Steuer werden auch die Skeptiker unter den passionierten Autofahrern ihr Herz an den 190 SL verlieren. Denn die Mercedes-Benz-Konstrukteure wissen ganz genau, wie sich die Freunde des sportlichen Fahrens und der individuellen Automobile den „Kommandostand" ihres Wagens wünschen. Das elfenbeinfarbene Lenkrad mit dem praktischen Signal- und Blinkring liegt zuverlässig griffig in der Hand, und die Rechte gelangt wie von selbst auf den kurzen sportlichen Schaltknüppel des Viergang-Getriebes. Im direkten Blickfeld finden Sie die großen, klaren Zifferblätter von Tachometer und Drehzahlmesser; darunter sind die Meßuhren für Kühlwassertemperatur und Öldruck angeordnet, und in bequemer Nähe liegen die Bedienungsknöpfe und -hebel. Nichts beeinträchtigt die ausgezeichnete Sicht durch die großflächige, gewölbte Windschutzscheibe, die selbstverständlich aus Verbundglas besteht. Die angenehme Sitzposition durch die richtig geformten Sitze macht das Fahren im 190 SL vollends zum sportlichen Vergnügen. Die großzügige Ausstattung wird ergänzt durch die Lichthupe, einen geräumigen, verschließbaren Handschuhkasten mit Zeituhr im Deckel, 2 gepolsterte Sonnenblenden (im Gegensatz zur Abbildung auch beim Roadster), Lenkschloß, Kartenleselampe und Innenspiegel. Und zur „inneren" Sicherheit ist das Armaturenbrett über die ganze Breite an der Ober- und Unterseite gepolstert. Am Lenkrad des 190 SL entdecken Sie die liebevolle Mühe, mit der man selbst das scheinbar Nebensächliche durchkonstruiert hat – und es wird Ihnen bewußt, daß der 190 SL in jeder Beziehung hält, was sein Äußeres verspricht.

Heizung und Lüftung

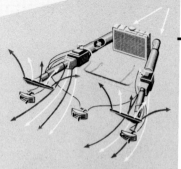

Wettersorgen haben Sie im 190 SL nicht, denn Fahrer und Begleiter können unabhängig von einander für ihren Platz das Klima schaffen, das ihnen am meisten behagt. Vom Sitz aus ist die Frischluftzufuhr in Temperatur, Menge und Verteilung (zum Fußraum oder gegen die Windschutzscheibe) fein einstellbar. Im Stand oder bei langsamer Fahrt sorgt das serienmäßige Entfrostergebläse für schnelle, angenehme Heizung des Innenraums.

Safety from the Ground Up

The heating of the 190 SL was very good too-which could not be said of many sports cars of that time . . .

„Sicherheit von Grund auf" war der Leitgedanke bei seiner Konstruktion: das Resultat ist eine seltene Harmonie von Sicherheit, Leistung und Komfort, die Sie mit Ihrem 190 SL erhalten. Seine Sicherheit beginnt mit der Stabilität der Rahmenboden-Anlage, einer außerordentlich verwindungssteifen und dabei hochelastischen Konstruktion. Sicherheit, wie sie für einen schnellen Wagen entscheidend ist, erhält Ihr 190 SL auch durch die Eingelenkpendelachse und die unabhängig aufgehängten Vorderräder. Der besonders tiefliegende Schwerpunkt trägt noch zu dem ausgezeichneten Fahrverhalten dieses sicheren Wagens bei, und seine große Wendigkeit wird voll wirksam durch die besonders leichtgängige Kugelumlauflenkung mit automatischer Nachstellung und Lenkungsstoßdämpfer. Das Beruhigendste aber – zumal für schnelle Fahrer – sind die turbogekühlten Bremsen mit der imponierenden Bremsfläche von 1064 qcm. Sie arbeiten stets zuverlässig, kraftvoll und ohne das gefürchtete „Fading", das Nachlassen der Bremswirkung. Dank des serienmäßigen ATE-Bremsgerätes ist nur ungefähr die Hälfte der Kraft erforderlich, mit der sie normalerweise die Bremsen bedienen müßten. Alle diese Vorzüge tragen dazu bei, daß Sie die hohe Leistung Ihres 190 SL nutzen können, wann und wo Sie es immer wünschen.

Sicherheit von Grund auf

Behind its steering wheel, even the skeptics among passionate car drivers will lose their hearts to the 190 SL. For the Mercedes-Benz constructors know very precisely how fans of sporty driving and of individual automobiles want the "command post" of their cars to be. The ivory-colored steering wheel with the practical horn and flasher ring is dependably at hand, and the right hand moves naturally to the sports-type stick shift of the four-speed transmission. Directly in your field of vision you find the large, clear dials of the speedometer and tachometer; underneath are the gauges for water temperature and oil pressure, and conveniently nearby are the control knobs and levers. Nothing hinders the excellent view through the large-surface bowed windshield, which is, naturally, made of laminated glass. The pleasant seating position, thanks to the correctly shaped seats, makes riding in the 190 SL a complete sporting pleasure. The array of controls is completed by the flasher lights, a roomy locking glove compartment with a clock on its lid, two padded sun visors (unlike the illustration, the Roadster has them too), a steering lock, map reading lamp and interior mirror. And "for inner" safety the dashboard is padded along its upper and lower edges for its entire length. At the wheel of a 190 SL you discover the loving car with which even the seemingly unimportant features have been made-and you become aware that the 190 SL keeps every promise that its exterior makes.

Heating and Ventilation

You have no weather problems in the 190 SL, for the driver and passenger can independently create the climate that suits them best for their areas. From each seat, the fresh air flow can be finely controlled as to temperature, quantity and division (to the foot space or against the windshield). When standing or driving slowly, the standard defroster blower provides for the quick, pleasant warming of the interior.

Rahmenboden-Anlage

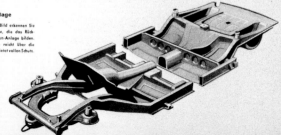

In dem nebenstehenden Bild erkennen Sie die soliden Kastenprofile, die das Rückgrat für die Rahmenboden-Anlage bilden. Dieser sichere Unterbau reicht über die ganze Wagenbreite und bietet vollen Schutz.

Fahrschemel und Eingelenkpendelachse

Der Hochleistungsmotor Ihres 190 SL ist mit dem Getriebe, der Vorderradaufhängung und der Lenkung im „Fahrschemel" zusammengefaßt. Diese praktische Lösung ermöglicht kostensparendes Aus- und Einbauen des ganzen Aggregats zu Wartungszwecken und dämpft außerdem etwaige Restschwingungen der Vorderradfederung. Die Eingelenkpendelachse hinten mit nur einem tiefgelegten Drehpunkt wird durch zwei Längslenker geführt. Große eigenreibungsfreie Schraubenfedern fangen jeden Fahrbahnstoß ab, ehe er sich auswirken kann.

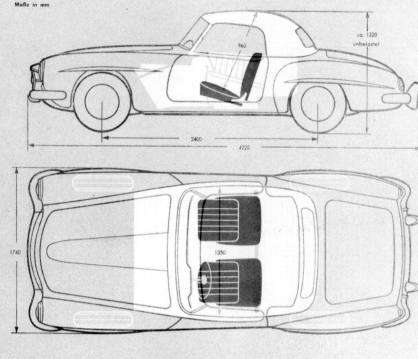

TECHNISCHE DATEN

Maße in mm

Printed in Germany   Ex P 243   459 de

Motor

Zahl der Zylinder	4
Bohrung/Hub	85/83,6 mm
Gesamthubraum effektiv	1897 ccm
Motorleistung *	120 gr. HP/5800 U/min nach SAE
	105 PS/5700 U/min nach DIN
Drehzahl bei 100 km/std	3370 U/min
Höchstdrehzahl	6000 U/min
Verdichtung	8,5:1
Vergaser	2 Solex-Register-Flachstromvergaser
Ölkühlung	Öl-Wasser-Wärmetauscher
Ölfüllung des Kurbelgehäuses	max./min. 4/2,5 Ltr.

Fahrwerte

Höchstgeschwindigkeit (je nach Aufbau)	
im 1. Gang	ca. 50 km/std
im 2. Gang	ca. 76 km/std
im 3. Gang	ca. 120 km/std
im 4. Gang	ca. 170–180 km/std
Steigfähigkeit	
im 1. Gang	ca. 50 %
im 2. Gang	ca. 30 %
im 3. Gang	ca. 17 %
im 4. Gang	ca. 9,5 %

Kraftstoff

Fahrverbrauch bei durchschnittlichen Überlandfahrten	ca. 8,2–12,3 Ltr./100 km
Kraftstoffverbrauch nach DIN 70030 **	10,9 Ltr./100 km (gemessen bei 110 km/std)
Oktanzahl des Kraftstoffes	Die Werkseinstellung des Motors erfolgt mit handelsüblichem Superkraftstoff von OZ 92 bis 93 nach der Research-Methode (ROZ)
Tankinhalt	65 Ltr.
davon Reserve	ca. 6 Ltr.

Fahrgestell

Wechselgetriebe	DB-Vierganggetriebe, zwangsvollsynchronisiert, Knüppelschaltung
Hinterachsübersetzung	1:3,9
Räder	5 K x 13 unsymmetrisch
Reifengröße	6,40–13 Spezial RS
Batterie	12 V, 56 Ah
Bremsanlage	Bremstrommeln mit Turbokühlung Bremsbacken mit automat. Nachstellung, ATE-Bremsgerät

Maße und Gewichte

Größte Länge	4220 mm
Größte Breite	1740 mm
Größte Höhe, unbelastet (mit Verdeck)	1320 mm
Radstand	2400 mm
Spurweite vorn	1430 mm
Spurweite hinten	1470 mm
Bodenfreiheit	ca. 155 mm
Wendekreisdurchmesser	ca. 11 m
Fahrzeuggewicht fahrtfertig mit Reserverad und Werkzeug	1140 kg
Zulässiges Gesamtgewicht	1400 kg
Nutzlast	260 kg

* Die angegebene Leistung in PS ist, da alle Nebenleistungen bereits abgezogen sind, an der Kupplung für den Antrieb des Wagens effektiv verfügbar.

** Ermittelt bei ¾ der Höchstgeschwindigkeit (max. 110 km/std) unter Zuschlag von 10 %.

Änderungen in Konstruktion und Ausstattung vorbehalten.

---

m the ground up" was the dominant concept in its design;
s a rare harmony of safety, performance and comfort that
with your 190 SL. Its safety begins with the stability of its
om chassis, and extraordinarily flex-free and yet highly
struction. Safety that is decisive for a fast car is also
by the 190 SL thanks to its single-joint swing axle and
tly suspended front wheels. The particularly low-lying
ravity also contributes to the excellent handling of this safe
great agility becomes fully effective through its especially
ulating-ball steering with automatic return and steering
he most comforting feature, though-especially for fast
s turbo-cooled brakes with the impressive braking surface
are centimeters. They always work reliably, strongly and
e dreaded "fading", the decrease of braking effect. Thanks
dard ATE power brake system, only half the strength is
with which you would normally have to operate the brakes.
vantages contribute to letting you use the high performance
SL whenever and wherever you want.

om Chassis

cture you can see the solid box profile that forms the
of the frame-bottom chassis. This safe foundation extends
ll width of the car and offers full protection.

nd Single-Joint Swing Axle

performance motor of your 190 SL is united with the
on, the front suspension and the steering in this
h". This practical solution allows economical removal and
t of the entire aggregate for service and also decreases the
of vibration from the front wheels. The single-joint swing
rear, with just one low-lying turning point, is led by two
al links. Large friction-free coil springs smooth out every
ne road before it can have any effect.

Only a few cars comparable to the 190 SL could offer such a large amount of space. Catalog page from 1959.

From a small collective brochure for the entire Mercedes-Benz passenger car program of 1957. The 190 SL takes an important place.

Typ 190 SL

Der rassige Tourensportwagen der Mittelklasse

Coupé

Mit seinem rassigen Kühlergesicht und dem eleganten Schwung der schnittigen Karosserie ist dieser temperamentvolle Wagen eine vollkommene „lebendige" Komposition. Ein Vierzylinder-Kurzhubmotor mit der Leistung von 105 PS beweist vom Start weg sein sprühendes Temperament. Durch geschwindigkeit von ca. 170 bis 18.. diesem reizvollen Wagen im dich.. Ausfahren der Endgeschwindigke.. erfahrungen entwickelten Kons.. Damit ist Ihre Sicherheit gewäh.. Fahrt mit diesem vielbewunder..

Type 190 SL
The thoroughbred middle-class touring sports car Coupe

7 Fasteners hold the light metal roof securely on the body. After loosening the toggles and screws, the coupe roof can be removed. Thus with a few twists the completely closed coupe becomes an elegant roadster.

With its thoroughbred radiator grille and the elegant lines of its stylish body, this spirited car is a completely "live" composition. A short-stroke four-cylinder motor that produces 105 HP shows its effervescent temperament from the start. With its fast acceleration, a top speed of about 170 to 180 kph, and its handling, in this charming car you are always at the front, even in the heaviest traffic. And even at its top speed, the 190 SL-thanks to its construction, developed from racing experience-remains firmly and accurately on course. This guarantees your safety, and you can enjoy every moment of a trip in this much-admired touring sports car in complete peace.

„Ein Mercedes-Benz"

Lob und Bewunderung klingen mit, wann immer man diesen Namen nennt. Im Aussehen wie in seinen Eigenschaften kündet jeder Mercedes-Benz von der schöpferischen technischen Leistung der ältesten Automobilfabrik der Welt und von den Erfahrungen aus zahllosen Sportsiegen. Mit ihrem umfassenden Angebot erfüllt die Daimler-Benz AG eine weite Skala individueller Wünsche nach ebenso leistungsfähigen wie eleganten Fahrzeugen. Der Mercedes-Stern gilt in aller Welt als Wahrzeichen für Sicherheit und Schnelligkeit, für Schönheit und gediegenen Komfort bei einem Automobil.

Typ 190 S

Roadster

AUF ALLEN STRASSEN

talldach
ösen der
...ung ist
... wird aus
... mit we-
Roadster.

..., eine Spitzen-
...it liegen Sie mit
... Und selbst beim
... seiner aus Renn-
...au auf der Bahn.
...en Augenblick der
...er Ruhe genießen.

MERCEDES-BENZ

...zum Verlieben

Dieser Wagen erwidert spontan Ihre Sympathie. Er tut alles, um Ihre Bequemlichkeit auch während einer langen Reise vollkommen zu machen; und in dem für einen Tourensportwagen sehr großen Kofferraum reist auch Ihr umfangreiches Gepäck bequem und sicher mit.

Als Coupé oder als Roadster — immer haben Sie mit dem 190 SL auch seinen Raum- und Fahrkomfort mitgewählt: Sicheren Halt geben die bequemen Polstersitze, und im Fond kann auf Wunsch ein dritter Sitz quer zur Fahrtrichtung eingebaut werden. Die auf jeder Seite des Armaturenbretts getrennt einstellbare Heizung und Lüftung sorgt stets für angenehmes Klima. Weitere Annehmlichkeiten, wie ein ATE-Bremsgerät, Entfroster- und Heizgebläse, Lichthupe und Starktonhorn, geben dem 190 SL die Ausstattung eines komfortablen Tourenwagens. Auf dem Armaturenbrett finden Sie alle Instrumente und Bedienungshebel so blick- und handgerecht angeordnet, daß Sie sofort mit ihnen vertraut sind.

"A Mercedes-Benz"

Praise and admiration are heard whenever one mentions this name. In its looks as in its characteristics, every Mercedes-Benz proclaims the creative technical achievement of the world's oldest automobile factory and its experiences from countless sporting victories. With their inclusive offerings, the Daimler-Benz firm fulfills a wide range of individual wishes for cars that are as capable as they are elegant. All over the world the Mercedes Star is a guarantee of safety and speed, beauty and luxurious comfort in an automobile.

Type 190 SLA Car for Falling in Love
Roadster

This car spontaneously responds to your emotions. It does everything to make your comfort complete, even during a long trip; and in the luggage space, very large for a touring sports car, your capacious luggage also rides along easily and safely.
As a coupe or a roadster-with the 190 SL you have always chosen its spacious driving comfort too; the comfortable upholstered seats hold you safely, and if you wish, a third seat can be installed transversely in the back. The heating and ventilation, adjustable separately at either side of the dashboard, always provides a pleasant climate. Further amenities, like ATE power brakes, defroster and heater vents, flashers and strong-tone horn, give the 190 SL the equipment of a comfortable touring car. On the dashboard you find all the instruments and controls arranged for easy viewing and handling, so that you are at home with them immediately.

Interested in a Real Bargain?

This 1959 brochure is a curiosity. It addresses British soldiers stationed in Germany, but the photos were taken at an American air base. Some of the cars bore American plates.

With American Features for the English

Model 190 SL

2 door, 2—3 passenger sports convertible or hard top coupé with four-cylinder ohc petrol engine, power assisted brakes, maximum cruising speed 110 mph.
£ 1269/ 5/- ex-factory as roadster,
£ 1315/ 8/- as coupé, and
£ 1357/15/- as removable hard top coupé with additional convertible top.

white wall tyres extra

96704

Factory photo of a 190 SL. The styling is timelessly elegant-no wonder that the car is still a desirable collector car today.

This picture too (opposite page) is one of a series that Daimler-Benz had taken in 1958 for advertising and press uses.

Elegance and Good Breeding

Though the front end of the 190 SL was styled after that of the 300 SL, the rear had acquired its own characteristic shape.

Until the 1959 model year, the hardtop had a small rear window. The size was regarded as sufficient then!

Roadster

The 190 SL is described as a touring sports car. Sport is to be understood in the original meaning of the word: derived from the Latin "disportare", meaning relaxation-and simultaneously as preparation for a new personal excitement. With this car you do not simply drive from A to B.. through a film-like backdrop, flashing up and disappearing again, of forests and villages, meadows and fields-rather you experience the landscape directly. In the process the 190 SL, though a car for demanding drivers, does not make any particular demands on your driving skill. It is easy to drive, because its roadholding is splendid, thanks to its independent suspension of all four wheels and its low center of gravity. because the steering reacts precisely to your slightest touch, and because in any situation a great reserve of driving power is at your disposal-a car for people who enjoy driving.

Roadster

With a few twists the roadster becomes a closed car without losing any of its elegant styling. With a single motion to the front, the roof is drawn to the upper edge of the windshield and fastened there with two toggles. This produces not a drafty and dripping "tent" but rather a weatherproof roof under which one drives on, cozy and protected from rain, snow and wind.

Der 190 SL wird als Tourensportwagen bezeichnet. Sport will dabei im Ur-Sinn des Wortes verstanden sein: vom lateinischen disportare her als Entspannung — gleichzeitig als Bereitschaft zu einer neuen, einer persönlichen Spannung. Mit diesem Wagen fahren Sie nicht einfach von A nach B, vorüber an einer filmartig aufblendenden und wieder verschwindenden Kulisse von Wäldern und Dörfern, von Wiesen und Äckern — Sie erleben vielmehr die Landschaft unmittelbar. Dabei stellt der 190 SL, obwohl ein Automobil für anspruchsvolle Fahrer, von sich aus keine besonderen Ansprüche an Ihre Fahrkunst. Er fährt sich leicht, weil seine Straßenlage dank der unabhängigen Aufhängung aller vier Räder und dank dem tiefen Schwerpunkt vorzüglich ist, weil die Lenkung auf Ihre leiseste Bewegung exakt reagiert und weil in jeder Situation eine große motorische Kraftreserve zu Ihrer Verfügung steht — ein Automobil für Menschen, die Freude am Fahren haben.

The folding top of the 190 SL was of good quality-rain and wind had no chance to bother the passengers . . .

Mit wenigen Handgriffen wird aus dem Roadster ein geschlossener Wagen, der damit nichts von seiner eleganten Linie verliert. Mit einer einzigen Bewegung nach vorn

wird das Verdeck bis an die Oberkante der Windschutzscheibe gezogen und dort mit den beiden Knebelverschlüssen befestigt. Das ergibt nicht etwa ein

zugiges und tropfendes »Zelt«, sondern ein wetterfestes Dach, unter dem man geborgen und geschützt gegen Regen, Schnee und Wind weiterfährt.

Like a Well-tailored Suit

The 190 SL was a prestige car, an ideal second car for households in which the wife especially valued her own elegant, chic two-seater . . .

Coupé

Der 190 SL ist ein repräsentatives Automobil. Das zeigt er schon als Roadster. Den Punkt auf das I aber setzt das — wahlweise abnehmbare — Coupédach. Es bietet vollkommenen Wetterschutz, vor allem auch im Winter. In seiner ästhetisch vollendeten Linienführung unterstreicht es noch die sportliche Note des Fahrzeugs. — »Autos machen Leute«, hat einmal jemand das bekannte Sprichwort abgewandelt. Wer das übertrieben findet, der wird jedoch zugeben, daß ein schöner Wagen die Daseinsfreude des Besitzers steigert und damit — in gutem Sinne — sein Selbstgefühl hebt. Und wer im Leben etwas darstellt, der betont mit der Wahl gerade des 190 SL seine Persönlichkeit. — Der 190 SL »sitzt« wie ein gut gearbeiteter Maßanzug. Genauso werden Sie sich in ihm auch fühlen, in Ihrem Wagen, dessen Eleganz so selbstverständlich wirkt. Seine wahre Klasse aber werden Sie erst dann ganz auskosten, wenn Sie während der Fahrt viel von ihm verlangen. Auch der sehr anspruchsvolle Fahrer wird feststellen: Der 190 SL läßt ihn in keiner Situation im Stich.

Coupe

The 190 SL is an impressive automobile. It shows this as a roadster. But the coupe roof-removable whenever you wish-is the finishing stroke. It offers complete protection from the weather, especially in winter. In its aesthetically perfected styling it emphasizes again the sporting tone of the vehicle.-"Cars make the man", as someone once changed the well-known saying. Whoever finds this exaggerated will have to admit, though, that a beautiful car enhances its owner's joy of living and thus-in the good sense-raises his self-esteem. And whoever wants to say something about himself in life, stresses his personality with the very choice of the 190 SL.-The 190 SL "fits" like a well-sewn made-to-order suit. That is exactly how you will feel in it, in your car whose elegance comes across so naturally. But you will really feel its true class when you demand much of it during a trip. Even the very demanding driver will see: the 190 SL does not leave him in the lurch in any situation.

Ein Testbericht über den 190 SL schloß mit den Worten: »Wer ihn einmal gefahren hat, wird sich nicht mehr von ihm trennen können.« — Zu den vielen Vorzügen dieses Automobils gehört, daß man sich vom ersten Augenblick an hinter seinem Lenkrad zu Hause fühlt. Alle Bedienungsorgane liegen griffgerecht, alle Kontrollinstrumente gut im Blickfeld des Fahrers: Gleich groß und übersichtlich sind Tachometer und Drehzahlmesser nebeneinander angeordnet, darunter Kühlwasser-Fernthermometer und Öldruckmesser. — Selbstverständlich ist der 190 SL mit Lichthupe, mit Scheibenwascher und mit Lenkschloß ausgestattet. — Das Zweispeichenlenkrad mit dem Signalring liegt paßgerecht und sicher in der Hand. Der Weg zum sportlich-kräftigen Schalthebel in der Wagenmitte unmittelbar vor den Sitzen ist gering — kurz, das »Cockpit« ist beides, schön und zweckmäßig. Der Tester hatte schon recht: Wer einmal auf diesem Platz gesessen hat, wer einmal diesen besonderen Wagen erlebt hat, der wird von diesem Automobil für immer begeistert sein!

This 190 SL catalog was spiral-bound as of 1960. The graphics faded into spacious white pages that corresponded to the elegance of the vehicle that the catalog advertised.

A test report on the 190 SL ended with the words: "Whoever has driven it once will never be able to part from it again."-Among the many advantages of this car is the fact that from the first moment on, one feels at home behind its steering wheel. All the controls lie close at hand, all the instruments are right in the driver's field of vision: equally large and clear are the speedometer and tachometer, set side by side, and under them the water thermometer and oil pressure gauge.-Naturally the 190 SL is equipped with flashers, windshield washers and a steering lock. The two-spoked steering wheel with the horn ring fits easily and securely in your hand. The distance to the sturdy sport-type gearshift in the middle of the car, just in front of the seats, is short-in brief, the "cockpit" is both beautiful and purposeful. The tester was right: whoever has sat in this seat once, whoever has experienced this particular car, will always be inspired by this car!

**At Home
Behind
the Wheel**

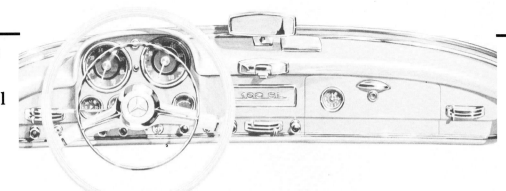

From 1955 to 1962 the dashboard remained as good as unchanged. The constancy of the model was even accepted by the American market . . .

Wer viel bei schlechtem Wetter unterwegs ist, weil er unterwegs sein muß, wer aber zugleich mit seinem besonderen Wagen, seinem 190 SL, in besonderer Weise repräsentieren will, der wählt das Coupé. Das jederzeit aufsetzbare und abnehmbare Dach mit der neuartigen zugfreien Dauerentlüftung macht aus dem »jugendlichen« Fahrzeug den Repräsentationswagen des Junggebliebenen. — Der vornehm unaufdringlichen äußeren Schönheit des Coupés entspricht die Innenausstattung von gediegener Eleganz, bei der jedes Einzelteil »vom Besten« ist. Polsterbezüge aus sorgfältig ausgesuchtem Leder bestimmen die Atmosphäre von kultivierter Behaglichkeit, zu der die handgerechte Anbringung von Ascher, Zigarrenanzünder, Kartenleselampe, Bedienungshebel für Lüftung und Heizung, von Fensterkurbeln und Türgriffen beiträgt. Eine Zeituhr in der Klappe des geräumigen, verschließbaren Handschuhfaches ist für Fahrer und Beifahrer gleich gut ablesbar. Das Wort Komfort wird hier groß geschrieben, und der Stil dieses Wagens zeigt sich auch in den Kleinigkeiten.

Das Coupédach, mit starken Gummiprofilen staubsicher abgedichtet, kann nach Lösen von Knebelgriffen und

Verschraubungen abgenommen, werden. So verwandelt sich das repräsentative Coupé in den eleganten

Roadster mit — auf Sonderwunsch — vollversenkbarem Verdeck. Mit ihrem 190 SL besitzen Sie dann zwei Wagen.

Whoever is on the road a lot in bad weather because he has to be, and yet wants to represent himself in a particular way with his particular car, his 190 SL at the same time, chooses the Coupe. The roof, which can be installed or removed at any time, with its modern draft-free constant ventilation, turns the "youthful" vehicle into the impressive car of those who stay young. The tasteful, understated beauty of the coupe matches the luxuriously elegant interior decor, of which every individual detail is "the best". Seat covers of carefully chosen leather determine the atmosphere of cultivated comfort which is contributed to by the handy location of the ashtray, cigarette lighter, map reading lamp, heating and ventilation controls, window cranks and door handles. A clock in the lid of the roomy, locking glove compartment is equally easy for the driver and passenger to read. The word Comfort is capitalized here, and the style of this car is shown in small things too. The coupe roof, made dust-free by strong rubber edges, can be taken off after loosening the toggles and screws. Thus the impressive coupe turns into the elegant roadster with-optionally-fully lowering top. With your 190 SL you then own two cars.

The set of luggage made to measure for the 190 SL gave an exclusive touch. Such extras were part of an old Daimler-Benz tradition-they already were available for the prewar 500 K!

Without great trouble, the coupe became a roadster when one removed the hardtop. New for 1959: the large panoramic rear window.

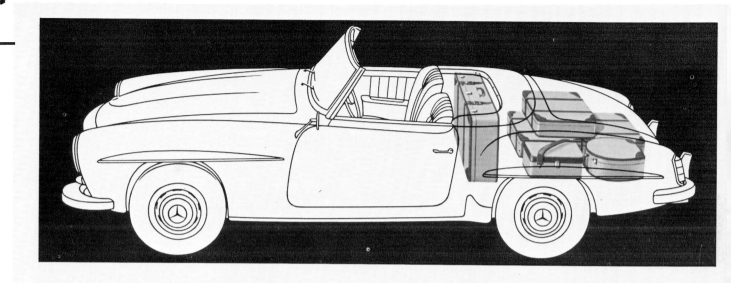

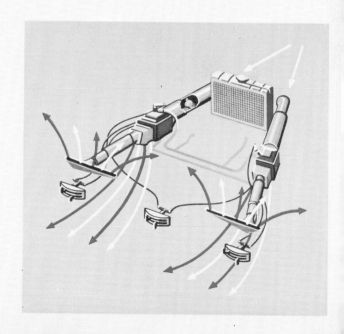

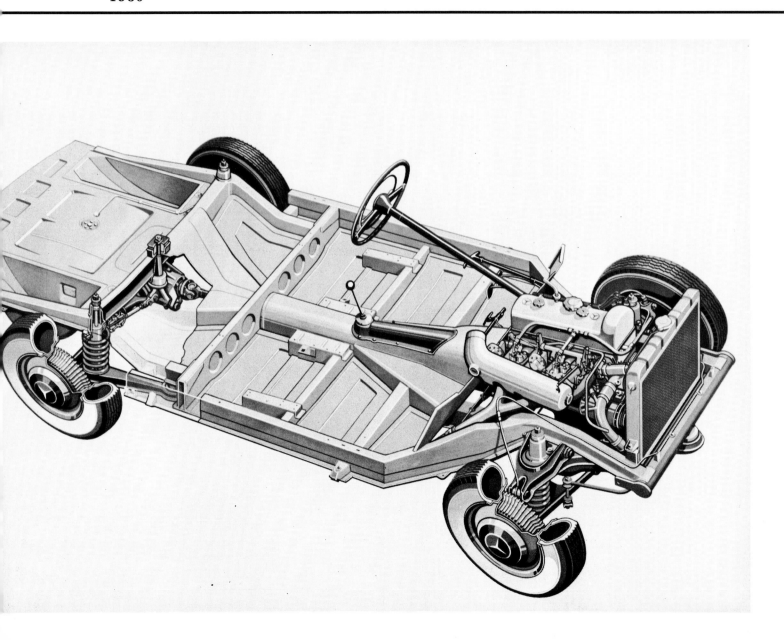

Safety from the ground up

The light touch of the Mercedes-Benz recirculating-ball steering returns automatically and keeps all road vibrations far from the driver with its steering damper.

The 190 SL is a beautiful, an elegant automobile, it is fast and full of verve. But these advantages only gain value and importance through the fact that the 190 SL is a safe car from the ground up. It is built on the renowned frame-bottom chassis, which along with the self-bearing body give the vehicle its extraordinary stability. Decisive for driving safety are the independent suspension and springing of the front wheels by transverse links and coil springs, its anti-sway characteristics thanks to its torsion-bar stabilizer; the low-lying turning point on the MB single-joint swing axle of the rear wheels, driven by hypoid gearing; the proven recirculating-ball steering and the turbo-cooled self-adjusting brakes that grip softly and yet powerfully without any dangerous fading. Thanks to the built-in servo brake, a good half of the necessary braking power is saved.

Have you already noticed the kind of impression people make who drive a 190 SL? You will hardly ever meet a 190 SL driver who sits at the wheel stiffly or looks bored. In fact, 190 SL drivers look happy and always give the impression of a positive outlook on life. Is that because of the car? Naturally, even the most beautiful car cannot make a satisfied person out of a grumpy one. But a beautiful, spirited car that it is fun to drive can, in fact-and the 190 SL is well suited to prove that-show its passengers the cheeriest side of life. One does not need to do very much, one just needs to be a little bit ready; then the 190 SL is more than just a beautiful car, it is a car that awakens the real joy of life.

The frame-bottom chassis provided great stability which lent the entire vehicle a considerable sturdiness.

Die leichtgängige Mercedes-Benz-Kugelumlauflenkung stellt sich automatisch nach und hält durch ihren Lenkungsstoß-dämpfer alle Fahrbahnstöße vom Fahrer fern.

Der 190 SL ist ein schönes, ein elegantes Automobil, er ist schnell und voller Temperament. Diese Vorzüge bekommen aber erst Wert und Gewicht dadurch, daß der 190 SL auch ein von Grund auf sicheres Automobil ist. Auch er ist auf der berühmten Rahmenbodenanlage aufgebaut, die in Verbindung mit der mittragenden Karosserie dem Fahrzeug seine außerordentliche Stabilität gibt. Entscheidend für die Fahrsicherheit sind die Einzelaufhängung und Abfederung der Vorderräder an Querlenkern und Schraubenfedern, ihre Neigungs-dämpfung durch den Drehstab-Stabilisator; der tiefliegende Drehpunkt der MB-Eingelenk-Pendelachse der Hinterräder mit Antrieb über Hypoid-Verzahnung; die bewährte Kugelumlauflenkung und die turbogekühlten, selbst nachstellenden Bremsen, die jederzeit ohne das gefürchtete Fading weich und doch kraftvoll greifen. Durch die eingebaute Servobremse wird gut die Hälfte der sonst notwendigen Bedienungskraft eingespart.

Haben Sie schon einmal darauf geachtet, wie die Menschen wirken, die einen 190 SL fahren? Nun, Sie werden kaum jemals einem 190 SL-Fahrer begegnen, der etwa steif oder auch nur gelangweilt am Lenkrad säße. Tat-sächlich wirken 190 SL-Fahrer fröhlich und bieten eigentlich immer den Eindruck einer positiven Einstellung zum Dasein. Ob das am Fahrzeug liegt? Natürlich kann auch das schönste Automobil aus einem Griesgram keinen vergnügten Menschen machen. Aber ein schöner, rassiger Wagen, in dem das Fahren Freude macht, kann doch — und der 190 SL ist wohl geeignet, das zu beweisen — seinen Insassen das Leben von der freund-lichsten Seite zeigen. Dazu braucht man gar nicht viel zu tun, man muß nur ein wenig bereit sein; dann ist der 190 SL mehr noch als ein schöner Wagen, dann ist er ein Automobil, das echte Freude am Dasein weckt.

The advertising texts from Daimler-Benz were always aimed at a precisely defined clientele. Here too, cultivated travel is stressed again-the 190 SL was scarcely seen as a racing car, as sporty as it looked.

Technical Data

Motor

Number of cylinders	4
Bore	85 mm
Stroke	83.6 mm
Displacement	1897 cc
Performance*	120 HP/5800 rpm (SAE) 105 HP/5700 rpm (DIN)
Top engine speed	6000 rpm
Compression	8.8:1
Carburetors	2 Solex horizontal Firing order1-3-4-2
Cooling/heating capacity	10 liters
Crankcase oil max./min.	4/2.5 liters

Statistics

Top speed in 1st gear	50 kph
2nd gear	76 kph
3rd gear	120 kph
4th gear	approx. 170-180 kph
Climbing ability in	
1st gear	50%
2nd gear	30%
3rd gear	17%
4th gear	9.5%

Fuel

Average open road fuel consumption: approx. 8.2-12.3 liters/100 km
Fuel consumption at 110 kph according to DIN 70030**: 10.9 liters

Fuel	Premium gasoline or gasoline-benzol mix
Tank capacity	65 liters
Reserve	approx. 6 liters

Transmission

Gearbox	DB 4-speed synchronized, stick shift
Rear axle ratio	3.9:1
Wheel size	5 K x 13 asymmetrical
Tire size	6.40-13 Sport
Battery	12-volt, 56 Ah
Brake system	Drums with turbo-cooling, self-adjusting brake shoes, servo brake

Weights

Weight ready to drive, with spare wheel, tools: 1140 kg
Allowable gross weight: 1400 kg

*Performance data in HP do not include power used by subsidiary aggregates not necessary to run the car. The listed performance in HP, with all subsidiary power already subtracted, is that effectively available at the clutch to propel the car. ** Produced at 3.4 top speed, max. 110 kph, plus 10%.

The ABC of Standard Equipment

Push-button starter
Padded armrests
Inset ashtray
Asymmetrical non-glare lightDirectional light control combined with horn ring
Directional lights under headlights and built into taillights
Directional indicator light set in dashboard
Boucle carpeting in the rear
Constant ventilation, draft-free, through rear louvers over the rear window of the coupe
Tachometer
High beam indicator light
Blower for heating and ventilation
Locking glove compartment
Rear lights including tail, stop, parking and back-up lights
Windshield and foot-space heating and ventilation, separate left and right controls
Interior light plus map reading light switched on by contact switch when driver's door opens, plus manually controlled
Instrument lighting
Map reading light
License plate lights built into bumper overriders
Trunk lighting by license plate light
Indicator light for directional lights and starter
Colling water thermometer
Fuel gauge with electric reserve indicator light
Painting, your choice of ten standard colors
Steering wheel with horn ring combined with directional control
Flasher light
Oil pressure gauge
Parking lights built into front directional and taillights
Upholstery, leather in coupe and coupe with roadster top, MB Tex in roadster
Spare wheel with bracket, standing at right side of trunk
Non-glare rear-view mirror
Seat backs separately adjustable to three positions
Seats longitudinally adjustable

Padded sun visors
Foot-operated windshield washer, combined with wipers
Overlapping two-speed windshield wipers
Strong-tone horn
Starter indicator light
Plug for hand light in engine compartment
Speedometer with overall and daily odometers
Locking fuel filler cap
Pockets in both doors, which are also door grips and armrests
Technology: see technical data*)
Doors can be locked from outside Tools in trunk
Windshield of laminated safety glass
Clock mounted in glove compartment lid
Cigarette lighter
Combined ignition and steering lock *) For exact listings of technical data, see above and on previous page

---

Technische Daten

Motor

Zahl der Zylinder	4
Bohrung	85 mm
Hub	83,6 mm
Gesamthubraum effektiv*	1897 ccm
Motorleistung*	120 gr. HP/5800 U/min nach SAE 105 PS/5700 U/min nach DIN
Höchstdrehzahl	6000 U/min
Verdichtung	8,8:1
Vergaser	2 Solex-Register-Flachstromvergaser
Zündfolge	1-3-4-2
Inhalt der Kühlanlage mit Heizung	10 Liter
Ölfüllung des Kurbelgehäuses max./min.	4/2,5 Liter

Fahrwerte

Höchstgeschwindigkeit

im 1. Gang	50 km/st
im 2. Gang	76 km/st
im 3. Gang	120 km/st
im 4. Gang	ca. 175 km/st

Steigfähigkeit

im 1. Gang	50%
im 2. Gang	30%
im 3. Gang	17%
im 4. Gang	9,5%

Kraftstoff

Fahrverbrauch bei durchschnittlichen Überlandfahrten .. ca. 8,2—12,3 Liter/100 km
Kraftstoffverbrauch nach DIN 70030**
gemessen bei 110 km/st .. 10,9 Liter/100 km

Kraftstoff	Superkraftstoff bzw. Benzin-Benzolgemisch
Tankinhalt	65 Liter
Reserve	ca. 6 Liter

Fahrwerk

Schaltgetriebe	DB-Viergang-Getriebe, zwangssynchronisiert, Knüppelschaltung
Hinterachsübersetzung	1:3,9
Felgengröße	5 K × 13 unsymmetrisch
Reifengröße	6,40—13 Spo
Batterie	12 V, 56 A
Bremsanlage	Bremstrommeln mit Turbo kühlung, Bremsbacken m automat. Nachstellung, Servobrem

Gewichte

Fahrzeuggewicht, fahrfertig mit Reserverad und Werkzeug Roadster	1140 k
Zulässiges Gesamtgewicht	1400 k

* Bei der Leistungsangabe in gross-horsepowe sind die Leistungen der zum Motorbetrieb nic erforderlichen Nebenaggregate unberücksic tigt. Die angegebene Leistung in PS ist, da al Nebenleistungen bereits abgezogen sind, e der Kupplung für den Antrieb des Wager effektiv verfügbar.

** Ermittelt bei ³/₄ der Höchstgeschwindigke max. 110 km/h, zuzüglich 10%.

ABC der serienmäßigen Ausstattung

Anlasser mit Druckknopfbetätigung
Armlehnen gepolstert
Aschenbecher, versenkt angebracht
Asymmetrisches Abblendlicht
Blinkerbetätigung mit Signalring kombiniert
Blinklichter, vorn unter den Scheinwerfern angebracht, hinten in Heckleuchten eingebaut
Blinklicht-Kontrolleuchte, versenkt in der Armaturenanlage
Bouclé-Teppich hinten
Dauer-Entlüftung, zugfrei durch hintere Auslaßschlitze oberhalb des Heckfensters beim Coupé
Drehzahlmesser
Fernlicht-Kontrolleuchte
Gebläse für Heizung und Lüftung
Handschuhkasten, verschließbar
Heckleuchten, enthaltend: Schlußlicht, Stopplicht, Parkleuchten und Rückfahrscheinwerfer
Heizung und Lüftung für Windschutzscheibe und Fußraum, rechts und links getrennt regulierbar
Innenbeleuchtung gleichzeitig Kartenleselampe, einschaltbar durch Kontaktschalter beim Öffnen der Fahrertür u. manuell verstellbar

Instrumentenbeleuchtung
Kartenleselampe
Kennzeichenleuchte in den Stoßstangenhörnern eingebaut
Kofferraumbeleuchtung durch Kennzeichenleuchte
Kontrolleuchte für Blinker und Starter
Kühlwasser-Fernthermometer
Kraftstoff-Vorratsanzeiger mit elektr. Reserve-Hinweis-Leuchte
Lackierung, Auswahl unter zehn Serienfarben
Lenkrad, mit Signalring und kombinierter Blinkerbetätigung
Lichthupe
Öldruckmesser
Parklicht in vordere Blink- und hintere Heckleuchten eingebaut
Polsterung, Leder beim Coupé und Coupé mit Roadster-Verdeck, MB Tex beim Roadster
Reserverad mit Halterung, rechts stehend im Kofferraum angeordnet
Rückblickspiegel, abblendbar
Rücklehnen der Einzelsitze in drei Schräglagen verstellbar

Sitze in Längsrichtung verstellbar
Sonnenblenden gepolstert
Scheibenwascher mit Fußbetätigung, kombinier mit Scheibenwischer
Scheibenwischer mit sich überschneidendem Wischfeld, zweistufig regelbar
Starktonhörner
Starter-Kontrolleuchte
Steckkontakt für Handlampe im Motorraum
Tachometer mit Gesamt- und Tageskilometerzähler
Tankdeckel verschließbar
Taschen an beiden Vordertüren, gleichzeitig Türziehgriffe und Armlehnen
Technik, siehe technische Daten*)
Türen, beide von außen verschließbar
Werkzeug im Kofferraum
Windschutzscheibe aus Sicherheits-Verbundglas
Zeituhr in Handschuhkastendeckel versenkt eingebaut
Zigarrenanzünder
Zündschloß mit Lenkschloß kombiniert

*) Genaue Angaben über technische Daten siehe oben und auf der Vorderseite

---

In February of 1963 the last 190 SL was built. The number of cars of this type built added up to 25,881.

Opposite page: At the same time as the 190 SL, the MGA was built (almost 100,000 of them) in England. Here is the first brochure for this sports car, from 1955.

The total of 25,881 190 SL cars sold surely does not justify speaking of "mass production", but the car was nonetheless a large-series vehicle. In its way the 190 SL was almost without competition, at least in Germany, for the Porsche was a "true" sports car, unlike the 190 SL, and the open version of the Borgward Isabella was a rarity on German roads even when it was in production. The competition from foreign firms in the SL category was stronger. One might mention the MGA, the Italian Lancia, the open version of the Peugeot 404, a masterpiece by Pininfarina, the Swedish Volvo 1000 (in coupe form), the Spider 2000 by Alfa Romeo. On the following pages are a few samples of advertisements for these cars, which were alternative choices for the sporty two-seater fan in the days of the 190 SL.

You have wished for it a long time-the MG in a new dress
Here it is-the new MG Series MGA

Das haben Sie sich schon lange gewünscht — den

MG IM NEUEN KLEID

MG SERIE **MGA**

Von diesem Wagen wird die Sportwelt morgen sprechen

Wir freuen uns, Ihnen das jüngste Glied der berühmten MG-Kette anbieten zu dürfen. Wie kaum ein zweites Unternehmen der Branche hat MG während 35 Jahren Erfahrungen im Sportwagenbau gesammelt. Die Summe dieser umfassenden Kenntnisse und das Bewusstsein, zuverlässige Mitarbeiter mit der verantwortungsvollen Aufgabe der Konstruktion betraut zu haben, ermöglichten überhaupt erst den Bau eines solchen Klassewagens.

We are happy to be able to offer you the newest link in the famous MG chain. Like scarcely any other undertaking of the firm, MG has gained experience in 35 years of sports-car building. The sum of this inclusive knowledge and the awareness of having entrusted reliable workers with the responsible job of construction has made possible the building of such a high-class car.
The sports world will be talking of this car tomorrow
The new MGA really deserves to be designated as the worthy successor to its world-famous forerunners.
New-but proven

Der neue MGA verdient es wirklich, als würdiger Nachfolger seiner weltbekannten Vorgänger bezeichnet zu werden.

Neu – aber bewährt

MG SERIE MGA

Safety fast !

Sicherheit trotz Geschwindigkeit

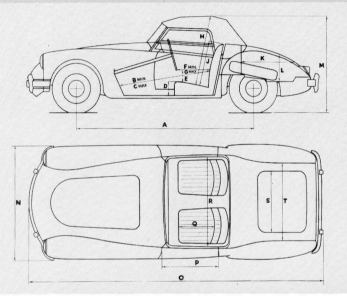

Abmessungen

A	B	C	D
239 cm	104 cm	119 cm	18 cm

E	F	G	H
15 cm	28 cm	43 cm	94 cm

J	K	L	M
53 cm	76 cm	36 cm	127 cm

N	O	P	Q
147 cm	396 cm	72 cm	47 cm

R	S	T	Gewicht
113 cm	76 cm	100 cm	875 kg

Spurweite vorn	Scheibenräder	1,206 m
	Speichenräder	1,216 m
Spurweite hinten	Scheibenräder	1,233 m
	Speichenräder	1,233 m
Bodenfreiheit		15 cm
Leergewicht approx.		875 kg

Safety despite speed
Measurements

Weight

Front trackDisc wheels	1.206 meters
Spoked wheels	1.216 meters
Rear trackDisc wheels	1.233 meters
Spoked wheels	1.233 meters
Ground clearance	15 cm
Approximate dry weight	875 kg

In the new model too, special value has been placed on good roadholding. To keep the center of gravity as low as possible, the box-section longitudinal members were lightly bowed so the seats would have room between the chassis members. The frame was also raised over the rear axle. It was not least on account of the aerodynamically designed styling that George Eyston was able to set many records. Just in August of 1954 he broke 8 international and 29 national American Formula F records.

Besonderen Wert legte man auch beim neuen Modell wieder auf eine gute Strassenhaltung. Um den Schwerpunkt möglichst tief lagern zu können, wurden die kastenförmigen Längsträger leicht ausgebuchtet, sodass die Sitze zwischen dem Chassisrahmen Platz fanden. Ausserdem wurde der Rahmen über die Hinterachse hochgezogen. Nicht zuletzt dank dieser aerodynamisch genialen Linienführung glückten George Eyston die zahlreichen Rekordfahrten. Allein im August 1954 brach er 8 internationale und 29 nationalamerikanische Rekorde der Formel F.

With the MGA the emphasis was much more clearly on sportiness. Under the long motor hood there was originally a 1.50 liter motor producing 69 HP.

61

Safe

Der MGA ist ein Wagen, den Sie persönlich besichtigen müssen. Setzen Sie sich ans Steuer, bedienen Sie die Gänge — fahren Sie! Nur so werden Sie erkennen, dass jede Einzelheit unter der schnittigen Karosserie zur Vollkommenheit dieses neuesten aller Sportwagen beiträgt.

The MGA is a car that you must see in person. Sit down at the wheel, shift the gears-drive! Only so will you recognize that every detail under the racy body contributes to the perfection of this newest of all sports cars.

The OHV 4-cylinder motor with a displacement of 1489 cc is equipped with two SU semi-downdraft carburetors, each with its own air filter. With scientific precision, unbeatable driving comfort was created, especially for long trips. The adjustable seats are covered in genuine leather.

Three very capacious suitcases can easily be carried in the big trunk. The spare wheel is also kept here.

The handy special steering wheel allows a clear view at the speedometer and tachometer. The upper rim of the dashboard is padded to protect the driver.

The proven independent front suspension with coil springs and swing struts guarantees absolutely vibration-free driving and first-class roadholding.

Der obengesteuerte Vierzylinder-Motor mit einem Hubvolumen von 1489 ccm ist mit zwei SU-Halbfallstromvergaser mit eigenem Luftfilter.

Mit wissenschaftlicher Gründlichkeit wurde besonders für lange Reisen ein unübertrefflicher Fahrkomfort geschaffen. Die verstellbaren Sitze sind mit echtem Leder überzogen.

Im grossen Kofferraum können mühelos drei sehr umfangreiche Gepäckstücke mitgeführt werden. Auch das Reserverad ist hier untergebracht.

Das sch...
des...

SPEZIFIKATIONEN

MOTOR: 4 Zylinder; Bohrung 73,025 mm; Hub 88,9 mm; Zylinderinhalt 1489 ccm. Obengesteuerter Motor mit Stösseln und Stosstangen und dreifach gelagerter Kurbelwelle. Kompressionsverhältnis 8,15 : 1. 69 PS bei 5500 U/Min. Wasserkühlung mit Pumpe, Ventilator und Thermostat. Druckschmierung durch Exzenterpumpe. Oelfilter im Hauptstrom. Inhalt der Oelwanne 3,7 l. Leichtmetallkolben mit 1 Oelabstreifer und 3 Kompressionsringen. 14 mm-Zündkerzen. Presstahl-Oelwanne.

BRENNSTOFFSYSTEM: 2 SU-Halbfallstromvergaser H4 mit einzelnen Luftfiltern; heckmontierte, elektrische SU-Hochleistungs-Benzinpumpe. Tankinhalt 45 l. Benzinuhr am Armaturenbrett.

ELEKTRISCHE AUSRÜSTUNG: 12 Volt-Zündung mit ölgefüllter Zündspule; Zündverteiler mit vollautomatischer Unterdruck- und Fliehkraft-Zündmomentverstellung; radio- und televisionsentstört; spannungsregulierender Dynamo, über Keilriemen angetrieben; Doppelscheibenwischer; Doppel-Schluss- und Stoplichter mit Blinkern für Richtungsanzeige; Fuss-Abblendschalter; separate Stadtlichter; Lucas-Doppelbatterien, gleichmässig hinter den Sitzen verteilt.

CHASSIS: Ausgesprochen robuste Kastenrahmenkonstruktion mit besonderer Torsionsfestigkeit; Chassisrahmen über die Hinterachse hochgezogen.

KRAFTÜBERTRAGUNG: Hydraulisch betätigte Einscheiben-Trockenkupplung Borg und Beck, 20 cm ⌀. 4 Vorwärtsgänge, 1 Rückwärtsgang. 2., 3. und 4. Gang synchronisiert. Gesamtübersetzungsverhältnisse: 1. Gang 15,652:1, 2. Gang 9,520:1, 3. Gang 5,908:1, 4. Gang 4,3:1.

Rückwärtsgang 20,468 : 1. Kurzer Getriebeschalthebel, in der Mitte angeordnet; Kardanwelle mit nadelgelagerten Kreuzgelenken.

HINTERACHSE: ³/₄-flottierende Hypoid-Hinterachse, Uebersetzung 4,3:1.

RADFÜHRUNG: Hinten halbelliptische Blattfedern mit hydraulischen Stossdämpfern. Unabhängige Vorderradführung mit Dreiecklenkern und Spiralfedern, hydraulische Stossdämpfer.

STEUERUNG: Direkte Zahnstangenlenkung; grosser Steuerraddurchmesser mit freier Sicht auf das Armaturenbrett. Nach Wunsch Rechts- oder Linkssteuerung.

BREMSEN: Hydraulische Lockheed-Bremsen auf alle 4 Räder. Durchmesser der Bremstrommeln 25,4 cm. Zentrale Handbremse mit Sicherungsknopf.

RÄDER: Gelochte Scheibenräder. Dunlopreifen 5,60 × 15.

INSTRUMENTE: Grosser Geschwindigkeitsmesser mit Höchstgeschwindigkeitsmarke; grosser Tourenzähler; Zündungslicht; Oeldruckmesser; Thermometer; Benzinuhr; Zündungsschalter; Instrumentenbeleuchtung mit veränderlicher Lichtstärke; Kartenleselampe; Schalter für Richtungsblinker; Lichtschalter.

KAROSSERIE: Offener, stromlinienförmiger Sportszweisitzer mit eingebautem Kofferraum; verstellbare Sitze, ganz mit echtem Leder überzogen; grosse Türfächer; Windschutzscheibe aus Sicherheitsglas; versenkbares, wasserdichtes Verdeck mit grosser Rückscheibe; abnehmbare Seitenfenster; Rückspiegel, in der Mitte über dem Armaturenbrett montiert; Reserverad, Werkzeug, Wagenheber und Andrehkurbel sind im Kofferraum untergebracht; Benzineinfüllstutzen mit Schnellverschluss; einteilige, nach rückwärts aufklappbare Motorhaube für leichte Zugänglichkeit zum Motor.

SPECIFICATIONS

MOTOR: 4 cylinders; Bore 73.025 mm, stroke 88.9 mm; displacement 1489 cc. Overhead-camshaft motor with tappets and rods and three crankshaft bearings. Compression ratio 8.15:1. 69 HP at 5500 rpm. Water cooling with pump, radiator and thermostat. Lubrication by eccentric pump. Mainstream oil filter. Oilpan capacity 3.7 liters. Light-metal rods with one scraper ring and 3 compression rings. 14-mm spark plugs. Pressed steel oilpan.

FUEL SYSTEM: 2 SU H-4 semi-downdraft carburetors with individual air filters; rear-mounted electric SU high-performance fuel pump. Tank capacity 45 liters. Fuel gauge on dashboard.

ELECTRICAL EQUIPMENT: 12-volt ignition with oil-bath coil; distributor with fully automatic operation; tension-regulating belt-driven dynamo; dual windshield wipers, dual tail-and stop lights with directional signals; foot dimmer switch; separate town lights; Lucas dual batteries, located behind the seats.

CHASSIS: Particularly robust box-frame construction with special torsion-firmness; chassis frame raised over the rear axle.

TRANSMISSION: Hydraulically activated single-plate Borg & Beck dry clutch, 20-cm diameter. 4 forward speeds, 1 reverse, 2nd, 3rd and 4th gears syncromesh. Gear ratios: 1st gear 15.652:1, 2nd gear 9.520:1, 3rd gear 5.908:1, 4th gear 4.3:1, reverse 20.468:1. Short stick shift mounted in the middle. Universal joint with needle-bearing cross links.

REAR AXLE: 3/4-floating hypoid rear axle; ratio 4.3:1.

SUSPENSION: Semi-elliptic rear leaf springs with hydraulic shock absorbers. Independent front suspension with triangular links and coil springs, hydraulic shock absorbers.

STEERING: Direct rack-and-pinion steering, large-dimension steering wheel with fine view of the dashboard. Optional right-or left-hand steering.

BRAKES: Lockheed hydraulic brakes on all 4 wheels. Brake-drum diameter 25.4 cm. Central hand brake with securing knob.

WHEELS: Pierced disc wheels. Dunlop 5.60x15 tires.

INSTRUMENTS: Large speedometer with top-speed mark; large tachometer; ignition light; oil pressure gauge; thermometer; fuel gauge; ignition switch; instrument lighting with variable brightness; map reading lamp; directional light lever; light switch.

BODY: Open streamlined sports two-seater with built-in trunk; adjustable seats covered in genuine leather; large door pockets; safety glass windshield; lowering watertight top with large rear window, removable side windows; rear-view mirror mounted centrally over the dashboard; spare wheel, tools, jack and crank stowed in the trunk; fuel filler with locking cap; one-piece motor hood raising backward for easy access to the motor.

Die bewährte, unabhängige Vorderradführung mit Spiralfedern und Schwinghebeln gewährt absolut erschütterungsfreies Fahren und erstklassige Strassenhaltung.

...t klare Sicht auf Ge... ...er. Der obere Rand ...der Fahrer gepolstert.

Despite its typically English appearance, the MGA shows design similarities to the Mercedes-Benz 190 SL. In its second model year, the performance of the British car increased to 72 HP, then to 80 and 86. The Type 1600 with dual overhead camshafts reached a high point of 108 HP, good for 180 kph.

Triumph T.R.3 Sports

The Triumph TR3 with 96 (later 101) HP was somewhat more rawboned than the MGA and more of a "sports car" in the classic sense. It was also a contemporary of the 190 SL.

Triumph T.R.3 Facts and Figures

GENERAL DIMENSIONS

Wheelbase	7 ft. 4 in.
Track Front and Rear (Disc Wheels)	3 ft. 9 in.
Front and Rear (Wire Wheels)	3 ft. 10 in.
	6 in.
Ground Clearance	35 ft.
Turning Circle	12 ft. 7 in.
	4 ft. 7½ in.
Overall Dimensions:	
Length	4 ft. 2 in.
Width	3 ft. 10 in.
Height (unladen):	
Top erect	3 ft. 4 in.
Top of screen	
Top folded and screen removed	
Baggage boot:	42 in.
Size of opening:	18 in.
Width	
Length	
Weight (Touring trim):	18¼ cwt.
Dry (excluding extra equipment)	19¾ cwt.
Complete (including tools, fuel, oil and water)	
	5.90-15 in. Dunlop
Tyres:	
Size	12 gals.
Capacities:	11 pts.
Fuel tank	1½ pts.
Engine sump	1½ pts.
Gearbox	13 pts.
Rear Axle	
Cooling system	

Consult your local distributor or dealer for the complete range of useful Stanpart accessory equipment that is available for this model.

PERFORMANCE

Engine: Maximum b.h.p. 100 at 5,000 r.p.m. Maximum torque 1,410 lb in. at 3,000 r.p.m. Equivalent to 145 lb sq. in. B.M.E.P.
Piston Speed (at vehicle's maximum road speed): 2,850 ft min. at 4,800 r.p.m. (This is equivalent to 100 m.p.h. in top gear.)
Maximum Speeds (Touring trim): Top gear, 110 m.p.h.

PETROL CONSUMPTION

Petrol Consumption	Constant Road Speed		
('Motor' Road Test Figures)	30 m.p.h. 48 km.p.h.	40 m.p.h. 64 km.p.h.	50 m.p.h. 80 km.p.h.
			38.0
m.p.g.	39.5	41.0	7.44
Litres 100 kms.	7.15	6.89	

Oil: 3,000 m.p.g.
Braking: 30 m.p.h. 30 ft. (under normal conditions). Stopping distance

	Speed	Time
Gear	20-40 m.p.h.	9 secs.
Top	30-50 m.p.h.	9 secs.
Acceleration (Two up):	0-50 m.p.h.	8 secs.
	0-60 m.p.h.	12 secs.
Through gears		18 secs.

Standing ¼ mile

COLOUR SCHEMES

Body Colour	Trim—(Leather or Vynide)
British Racing Green	Silverstone Grey or Red
Pale Yellow	Silverstone Grey, Red or Black
Black	Silverstone Grey, Red, Black or Blue
Signal Red	Silverstone Grey, Red or Black
Powder Blue	Black or Blue
Spa White	Silverstone Grey, Red, Black or Blue

N.B. Hood and Side Curtains—Black or White.
Hard Tops available in any T.R.3 body colour to produce single or two colour exterior.

OPTIONAL ITEMS AT EXTRA COST

Leather upholstery. Soft Top Kit (for Hard Top model). Heater. Wire wheels. Overdrive. Adjustable steering. Occasional Rear Seat. White Wall Tyres. Tonneau cover. Dunlop High Speed Tyres. Michelin X Tyres. Heavy Duty Tyres. (These should be fitted if the car is to be used regularly at speeds in excess of 90 m.p.h.) Windscreen washer. Two-speed screen wipers.

SOME OUTSTANDING SUCCESSES

IN EUROPE

Alpine Rally
1956 Team Award. Five Alpine Cups. 2,000 c.c. class, 1st, 2nd, 3rd, 4th and 5th.
1958 1,600 c.c.—Unlimited Class 1st, 2nd.
1959 2,000 c.c. and over—1st.
1,600-2,000 c.c.—1st, 2nd.

Liège-Rome-Liège
1957 2nd, 3rd and 5th places in the 1,300-2,000 c.c. class. Manufacturer's team prize. 3rd, 5th and 9th in General classification.
1958 1,601-2,000 c.c. 2,000 c.c. Class 1st.
1959 Over 1,600 c.c. Grand Touring Class, also Coupe des Dames.

Tulip Rally
1958 Normal Grand Touring Production Cars 1,600-2,000 c.c. 1st, 3rd.

England
1955 The R.A.C. Rally. Sports Car Class 1st.
General classification 2nd.

Scotland
1959 Scottish Rally Premier Award (Weir Trophy). Grand Touring Cars Class 1,601-2,000 c.c. and over, 1st, 2nd, 3rd.

Ireland
1955 Circuit of Ireland Trial 1st, 2nd and 3rd.
1956 Circuit of Ireland Trial 1st, 2nd, 3rd, 5th, 6th, 7th.
1958 Circuit of Ireland Trial 1st, 2nd and 3rd and Team Award.

France
1954 Le Mans 24-hour race. Competing against International type racing cars a privately entered Triumph Sports Car averaged 74.71 m.p.h. for 24 hours, with a fuel consumption of 34.7 miles to the gallon.
1955 Le Mans. A works entered team of three Triumph Sports all completed the course, the two leaders averaging almost 85 m.p.h. for the 24 hours.
1957 Tour de France. Coupe des Dames.

Belgium
1953 Jabbeke Highway, 124 m.p.h. in speed trim.
1956 Les Douze Heures de Nivelles 2,000 c.c. class, 1st and 2nd.

Germany
1956 Rally Trifels 2,000 c.c. class, 1st, 2nd and 3rd.

Italy
1959 At Monza, eight world time and distance records were broken by a production T.R.3, averaging speeds of over 100 m.p.h. for distances up to 5,000 miles. It was driven by members of the Cambridge University Automobile Club.

Corsica
1957 Rally of Corsica. Ladies' Prize.
1st in class, general classification.

IN THE U.S.A.

1954 Torrey Pines, stock over 1,500 c.c. 1st, 2nd, 3rd in class, 3rd overall. Race 14, all classes over 1,500 c.c. 1st in class, 3rd overall.
1955 Pebble Beach, Cypress Point Handicap, 1st, 2nd, 3rd in class, 5th overall, 3rd in class. Main Event.
1957 National, Elkhart Lake. 1st in class.

Triumph

The Triumph T.R.3 offers real comfort combined with outstanding performance. Both soft and hard top models are available. Speedometer and rev. counter are positioned directly in front of the driver for instant reference. The other instruments are neatly grouped in the centre panel of the facia. A lockable glove compartment surmounted by a grab handle occupies the passenger side of the facia. New form-hugging bucket type seats are adjustable fore and aft. The passenger seat folds forward to allow easy access to the rear stowage space which is padded and trimmed in pleated Vynide. Stubby type, remote control gear lever is well positioned for quick and positive gear changes; the hand brake is centrally mounted for convenience. External lockable handles in chrome finish are fitted to both doors and the luggage boot cover.

The Triumph T.R.3 has separate brake lights and flashing indicators. A chromium plated registration plate illuminator enhances the appearance. Side curtains that are easily installed and removed ensure an all-weather seal; fresh air ventilation is provided by the air intake on the scuttle. A saloon or open roadster at your will, conversion takes only a matter of seconds. Closed or open its sleek lines give a special eye appeal to this distinguished British sports car.

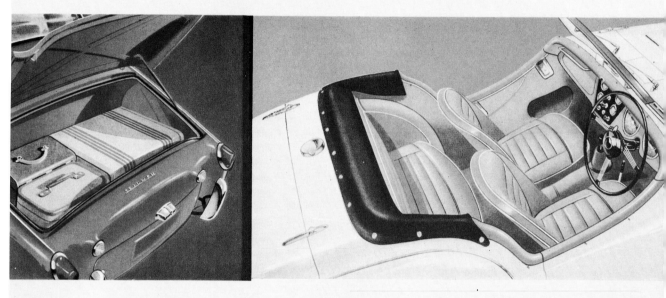

BODY

Luggage Accommodation—Space behind seats and in boot. Glove compartment in dash with lock. Spare wheel housed in separate compartment with locked panel below boot. Chrome handle on boot lid. The large, roomy luggage compartment is, in fact, the most spacious supplied with any sports car in its class and will hold more than enough luggage for extensive touring.

Upholstery—Vynide. (Leather as optional extra.)

Seating—Two bucket-type seats, adjustable fore and aft. The back of the passenger seat folds forward to give access to rear.

Instruments—5 in. tachometer and 5 in. speedometer with trip, positioned in front of driver. Separate instruments for fuel, water temperature, oil pressure and ammeter. Indirect instrument illumination. Ignition, direction indicator and headlamp high beam warning lights.

Controls—Buttons for starter, choke, windscreen wipers, fresh air ventilator, headlam and dash lights. Ignition lock.

Locks—Dovetail, anti-rattle type lock on both doors and boot with exterior chrome

Interior of car—The optional rear seat makes the Triumph T.R.3 a true family car. T can sit comfortably in the back, snug and safe. No doors to snap open, and the sides c high at the back seat for added safety.

CHASSIS

Engine—A four cylinder overhead valve power unit of 1991 c.c. The compression ra producing 100 B.H.P. at 5000 R.P.M. Bore 83 mm. Stroke 92 mm. Cylinder sleeves and fitted in direct contact with cooling water. Three bearing crankshaft with f hyposine camshaft.

The interior of the Triumph was tighter than the 190 SL, naturally. And the operation was not at all playful-the TR3 was something for ambitious drivers.

d for comfort with outstanding performance

	Top	3rd	2nd	1st	Rev.
	1.00	1.325	2.00	3.38	4.35
	Top	3rd	2nd	1st	Rev.
	3.7	4.9	7.4	12.5	16.1
otional extra):	3.03	4.02	6.07		

shaft—Hardy Spicer all-metal shaft, needle roller bearings. Short length to avoid implify frame construction.

—(Front)—Low periodicity independent suspension system with wishbone shackles ottom. Patented bottom bush and top ball jointed wheel swivels. Coil springs con telescopic dampers. Taper roller hub bearings. (Rear)—Wide semi-elliptic springs by piston type dampers.

Jacking—Mid-point side jacking.

Wheels—Steel disc type, silver finish, with chrome nave plates.

Brakes—Girling hydraulic. Front: caliper disc type. Rear: alloy cast iron brake drums incorporating leading and trailing shoes. Foot brake operates on all four wheels. Centrally mounted hand brake operates mechanically on rear wheels only.

Frame—Rigid structure, channel steel pressings braced by a cruciform member. Fully rust-proofed.

Steering—High gear, cam and lever type unit. Optional right or left-hand drive. Steering wheel 17 in. dia. three-spoke, spring type.

Battery—12 volt, 51 amp/hour located under bonnet.

alfa romeo

2000

spider   2 seats   2 doors

Alfa Romeo
2000 spider

Another picture-pretty car was the Alfa
Romeo 2000 Spider, introduced in 1957,
with its Superleggera body by Touring of
Milan. The car was built in small series
until 1961.

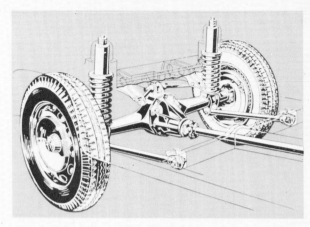

The flexibility of the **suspension** in the « 2000 Spider » is superb. The rubber pads have a progressive action and keep the car on an even keel, even on the most difficult bends.

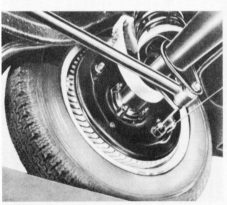

The **brake system** is typical Alfa Romeo: in front, the « 2000 Spider » has a two leading shoes brake type, while all the four drums are equipped with helicoidal fins for cooling.

technical features

Number of cylinders		4
Bore and stroke	mm	84.5 × 88
Piston displacement	cc	1975
Horsepower	HP 115	(HP-SAE 133)
Maximum revolutions	r.p.m.	5700
Front track		4' 7"
Rear track		4' 6"
Wheel base		8' 2"
Minimum turning circle		15' 9"
Overall length		14' 4"
Overall width		5' 5"
Overall height		2' 11"
Dry weight	lbs	2649
Fuel consumption	m.p.g.	20
Maximum speed	m.p.h.	109
Seats		2
Tyre size		165 × 400
Electrical system		12 Volt - 50 Amp. Hrs.
Fuel tank	gals	15.8

Clutch: single dry-plate, hydraulically operated.

Valve gear: inclined valves in the hemispherical cylinder head, cams acting directly on valve stems, spring cap oil cups, double overhead camshafts.

Gear-box: 5 synchronized forward speeds and 1 reverse. Ball gear shift lever.

Front suspension: independent with transverse linkage, coil springs, stabilizing bar and telescopic hydraulic shock absorbers. Rear suspension: rigid axle housing with upper triangular thrust rods and lower radius rods, coil springs, hydraulic and telescopic shock absorbers.

Differential: with hypoid bevel gears.

Left hand drive, by worm and roller.

Brakes: hydraulic, the front with two leading shoes; helical cooling fins on the drums.

The above data are only nominal

ALFA ROMEO S.P.A. · VIA GATTAMELATA, 45 · TELEFONO 39.77 · MILANO

D. C. Pro. 4 - 1959 (1)

Printed in Italy - Istituto Grafico Bertieri · Milano

The « 2000 Spider » is the outcome of the close cooperation between Alfa Romeo and Carrozzeria Touring. Provided with excellent features of roominess and comfort, it can attain with the utmost safety quite considerable a speed. It is therefore particularly suited for long and quick travels and for turing-purposes. The car side view presents an almost horizontal line, from head-lamps to the ends of the rear fins, conferring a tone of classic elegance. The low hood and the tapered fenders give the driver a perfect view of the full width of road. The two doors are front hinged for better safety and their large dimensions enable an easy access. The side windows may completely disappear into the bodies of the doors, while, when they are raised, they form a perfect flank with the windscreen line.

The luggage rear compartment is roomy and [...] the floor level, leaves the space for more luggage [...] matched range of new colours. On customers re[...] optional fittings, such as: the handle on the ins[...] with the same material as the inside upholstery [...] coverings in leather; different colourings from [...] top » of easy fit and perfectly harmonised with [...]

The high capacity battery gives ample power for starting from cold even under the most severe conditions. The headlights are of the very latest design with asymmetrical beams which give a high degree of visibility on the right hand side of the road when dimmed. The fog lights are incorporated in the parking lights. The tail lights are large and of modern design. The reversing lights are fitted in reflectors of ample dimensions.

The layout of the instrument panel is both elegant and functional. The instruments are arranged so that they can be instantly read without distracting the driver's attention from the road.
The instruments, switches and accessories, are non-reflecting and the upper part of the panel is padded for safety and covered with non-reflecting plastic material.
The external framing of the wind-shield and rear window is of stainless steel. The 5-Speed gear box shift is by central lever. The gear lever has been insulated from the engine-gear vibrations as well as the inside room has been insulated from noises. The car has two seats with valuable interior room. The seats can be shifted longitudinally, while their backs are of adjustable tilt type. The room behind the seats may be used for the extra luggage, exceeding the capacity of the rear compartment.

... wheel, under ... ler a perfectly ... ompleted with · ... senger, covered ... complete inner ... tones; · hard- ... on into a coupé.

4-cylinder engine with two overhead camshafts. The engine, in spite of its brilliant performances, is remarkably noiseless thanks to the valve gear with oil cups and to a special type of piston.
Another aid to silence is given by the use of aero-engine type exhaust valves which have a very low coefficient of expansion when under load. The engine is fed by two horizontal twin carburettors, Solex 44 PHH, with a throttle air-damped controlled by the inlet vacuum of the second stage.

The Italian convertible was pleasing from all sides with its chic styling. The 2-liter motor produced 115 HP at 5700 rpm (180 kph); the Alfa Romeo 2000 had a standard 5-speed gearbox.

VOLVO P 1800

The Volvo P 1800 is a car that attracts attention through the sheer beauty of its handsome lines and its effortless sparkling performance both in dense city traffic and on the open highway. The power unit in this graceful and luxurious car is a thoroughbred one hundred horse-power unit driving through a fully synchronized gearbox while the suspension is well in keeping with the technical perfection of the power system. The Volvo P 1800 is the natural choice of those who make outstanding demands on luxurious comfort, relaxed safety and complete reliability. The faultless road-holding qualities of this car together with safety details such as disc brakes on the front wheels, safety belts and padded dash-board make long-distance driving sheer enjoyment. To drive the Volvo P 1800 with its carefully planned interior appointments, clearly visible instrumentation and conveniently located controls is an exhilarating ex-perience. This car is also designed for varying climatic conditions since the body is very effectively rust-proofed and standard equipment includes a powerful heater-defroster and two separate air intakes as well as electric windscreen wipers and washers. The Volvo P 1800 makes your everyday driving a pleasure and your leisure motoring is the unique experience of handling a car with superb performance and with effortless power at your command.

Only at the end of 1960 did a competitor for the Mercedes-Benz 190 SL come on the market in Sweden. This was the Volvo P 1800 with its 90-HP four-cylinder motor. The car never became any too widespread in Germany.

73

a short presentation of the P

100 h.p. sports engine with twin carbur
Disc b
Braced-tread, 165-15 sports
12-volt b
Fully synchronized four-speed ge
Padded dash
Dazzle-free rear view r
Loud-tone
Headlight f
Overdrive (optional
Separate bucket
Two occasional
Parcel sh
Drum b

The Volvo P 1800, available only as a coupe, had two auxiliary seats behind the comfortable front seats, plus a respectable trunk. A vehicle of high individuality and proverbial durability.

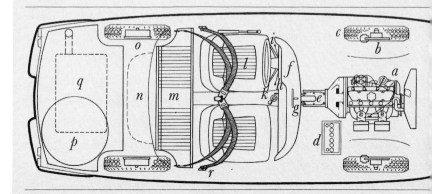

Spare

Isabella coupé

From February of 1957 to September of 1961 the Borgward Isabella Coupe was built in Bremen. A conservative, solidly built car without great sporting ambitions. Comparable to the 190 SL in design but less demanding in terms of technology.

BORGWARD *Isabella* coupé

Borgward Isabella Coupe
TECHNICAL DATA
Motor, carburetor, ignition
Cylinders in line, displacement 1493 cc, compression 8.2:1, 75 HP, maximum torque 11.6 mkg, 3580 rpm at 100 kph, Solex PA JTA carburetor, dropped valves, 6-volt electrical system, 70 Ah battery
Clutch and Gears
Hydraulic single-plate dry clutch, steering-wheel shift lever, 4 fully synchronized forward speeds, 1 reverse; ratios: 1st gear 3.86, 2nd 2.15, 3rd 1.36, 4th 1.0. Climbing ability: 1st gear 42%, 2nd 22%, 3rd 14%, 4th 11%
Suspension, Steering, Tires, Brakes, Signals
Self-bearing all-steel body, independent front suspension, rear swing axle, front and rear coil springs and telescopic shock absorbers; rear axle ratio 3.9:1, ZF rolling segment steering, 3 turns of steering wheel, 11-meter turning circle; tire size 5.90 x 13, RS tubeless; oversize brake surface 744 square cm, horn and flasher.

Performance and Consumption
Top speed approximately 150 kph, acceleration from zero to 100 kph in 18.5 seconds, fuel consumption according to DIN 70030 in newest form (testing speed 110 kph) ... 9.2 liters per 100 km.
Interior Space
Seat width from door to door 1.30 meters, individual seats with lowering backs; fresh air heating, standing heating, defroster on each side.
Weights and Measures
Allowable gross weight 1440 kg, performance weight 14.7 kg/HP, dry weight 1100 kg, length 4390 mm, width 1705 mm, height 1365 mm, wheelbase 2600 mm, front track 1336 mm, rear track 1360 mm, ground clearance 175 mm
Capacities
Fuel tank capacity 48 liters, oil capacity of crankcase 4.5 liters
Right to make construction and color changes reserved

76

TECHNISCHE DATEN

Motor, Vergaser, Zündanlage

4 Zylinder in Reihe; Hubvolumen 1493 ccm; Verdichtung 1 : 8,2; 75 PS; Max. Drehmoment 11,6 mkg; U/min bei 100 km/h = 3580; Registervergaser Solex PA JTA; Panzerventile hängend; Elektr. Anlage 6 V, Batterie 70 Ah

Kupplung und Getriebe

Hydraulische Einscheiben-Trockenkupplung; Lenkrad-Schaltung; 4 vollsynchr. Vorwärtsgänge, 1 Rückwärtsgang; Untersetzungen: 1. Gang 3,86, 2. Gang 2,15, 3. Gang 1,36, 4. Gang 1; Steigfähigkeit: 1. Gang 42%, 2. Gang 22%, 3. Gang 14%, 4. Gang 11%

Fahrwerk, Lenkung, Reifen, Bremsen, Signalanlage

Selbsttragd. Ganzstahlkarosserie; vorn Einzelradaufhängung, hinten Pendelachse; vorn und hinten Schraubenfedern und Teleskopstoßdämpfer; Hinterachs-Untersetzung 1 : 3,9; ZF-Rollensegment-Lenkung; Lenkrad-Umdrehungen 3,0; Wendekreis 11 m; Reifen 5,90×13, RS-schlauchlos; überdimensionierte Bremsfläche 744 qcm; Licht- und Schallhupe

Leistung und Verbrauch

Spitzengeschwindigkeit ca. 150 km/h; Beschleunigung von 0 auf 100 km/h 18,5 sek; Kraftstoffverbrauch nach DIN 70030 neueste Fassung (Prüfgeschwindigkeit 110 km/h) ... 9,2 ltr/100 km

Innenraum

Sitzbreite von Tür zu Tür 1,30 m; Einzelsitze mit Schlaflehnen; Frischluft-Heizung; Standheizung; Defroster, beidseitig

Abmessungen und Gewichte

Zul. Gesamtgewicht 1440 kg; Leistungsgewicht 14,7 kg/PS; Leergewicht 1100 kg; Länge 4390 mm; Breite 1705 mm; Höhe 1365 mm; Radstand 2600 mm; Spurweite vorn 1336 mm, hinten 1360 mm; Bodenfreiheit 175 mm

Füllmengen

Tankinhalt 48 Liter; Ölinhalt im Kurbelgehäuse 4,5 Liter

Konstruktions- und Farbänderungen vorbehalten

Diese neue Schöpfung ist ein sportlicher Wagen von wahrhaft mondäner Eleganz, ist „haute couture" in Stahl, Lack und blitzendem Chrom. Großzügig in seiner gesamten Konzeption, voller Anmut durch den Schwung seiner Linien und durch die aparten Farbkombinationen, ist das ISABELLA ...agen für Autofahrer, die an Eleganz ebenso hohe Ansprüche stellen wie an technische Voll- und Karosseriegestalter haben hier eine Synthese von Kraft und Schönheit geschaffen. Die ...LA COUPE läßt den starken Motor, der sich vieltausendfach schon bei der ISABELLA TS ...en. Die hervorragende Federung, die alle Unebenheiten der Fahrbahn auffängt, das ideale ...kt und die vollschwingende hintere Pendelachse sorgen für beste Straßenlage, für sichere ...dimensionierte Bremsflächen und schlauchlose Reifen sind weitere Faktoren der Sicherheit. ... ist auf höchste Ansprüche zugeschnitten. Lichthupe, elektrischer Scheibenwascher, kombi- ...Belüftung und Entfrostung, die griffgerechte Bedienungs-Tastatur, Parkleuchten links und ...g von COUPE und Kofferraum sind deshalb Selbstverständlichkeiten. Die Innenausstattung ...Details bietet einen nicht alltäglichen Komfort. Überaus bequem sind die mit viel Geschmack ...schaumgummigepolsterten Sitze mit ihren verstellbaren Rücklehnen, mit eingearbeiteten ...chmackvoll abgesetzte Bespannung der Seitenwände, der Bouclé-Teppich, mit dem der ganze ...hlagen ist, und viele andere Einzelheiten dienen dem Komfort und einer vornehmen Reprä- ...r rechten Sonnenblende eingearbeitet ist, bildet eine kleine Galanterie der Mitfahrerin gegen- ... besonders gedacht hat, bekundet ferner die Polsterung über dem Armaturenbrett. Sie dient ... der inneren Sicherheit. Alles in allem: Das ISABELLA COUPE ist ein Wagen, bei dessen ...tive zu verzichten. Man muß ihn sehen und probefahren. Das Übrige mag dann getrost

Das Herz des ISABELLA COUPE ist der temperamentvolle 75 PS-Motor, der sich schon bei ISABELLA TS (Touring Sport) viel-tausendfach bewährt hat. Er ist für sportliche Höchstbeanspruchung ebenso qualifiziert wie für touristische Dauerleistungen.

This new creation is a sporting car of truly fashionable elegance, it is "haute couture" in steel, paint and gleaming chrome. Superb in its whole design, full of grace through the sweep of its lines and its striking color combinations, the ISABELLA COUPE is a car for drivers who demand as much in elegance as in technical perfection. Constructor and bodywork builders have created a synthesis of power and beauty here. The flat, streamlined style of the ISABELLA COUPE allows the powerful motor, which has already proved itself in thousands of ISABELLA TS, unleash its full performance. The outstanding suspension that eliminates all the unevenness of the road surface, the ideal relationship between track and gravity, and the fully swinging rear swing axle provide the best handling and safe roadholding and cornering. Oversize brake surfaces and tubeless tires are additional safety factors. The ISABELLA COUPE is equipped to meet the highest demands. Flashers, electric windshield washer, combined heating, ventilating and defrosting system, handy controls, left and right parking lights and automatic interior lighting of the COUPE and trunk are to be taken for granted. The interior decor with its numerous lovingly created details offer more than everyday comfort. The foam-rubber upholstered seats, tastefully matched to the body color, are especially comfortable and have adjustable backs, side piping and headrests. The tasteful covering of the side walls, the Bouclé carpeting with which the whole car, including the trunk, is covered, and many other details provide comfort and make a fine impression. The make-up mirror, which is mounted in the right sun visor, offers a small favor to the lady passenger. The fact that special consideration has been given to the passenger is also shown by the padding over the dashboard. It not only offers comfort, but also safety inside. All in all, the ISABELLA COUPE is a car that it is hard to describe without using superlatives. One must see and test-drive it. The rest can then be left to your judgment.

The heart of the ISABELLA COUPE is its lively 75-HP motor that has already proved itself by the thousands in the ISABELLA TS (Touring Sport). It is just as highly qualified for sporting events as for long trips.

The 1.5-liter four-cylinder motor of the Isabella produced 75 HP, enough for a genuine top speed of 150 kph. An ideal long-distance runner, luxurious and comfortable.

Isabella cab...

Technical Data

Motor
4 cylinders in line
Three-point rubber mounting
Displacement 1493 cc
Bore 75 mm, stroke 84.5 mm
Compression 7:1
60 HP
Maximum torque 11 mkg
Mechanical fuel pump
Water cooling with thermostat and pump
Solex PJCB downdraft carburetor
Dropped valves
6-volt electric system, 84 Ah battery

Isabella TS, de Luxe, Coupé)
Compression 8.2:1
75 HP
Maximum torque 11.6 mkg
Solex PAJTA carburetor

Clutch and Gears
Hydraulic single-plate dry clutch
Steering column shift lever
4 fully synchronized forward gears
1 reverse gear
Gear ratios: 1st 3.86, 2nd 2.15, 3rd 1.36, 4th 1.0
Climbing ability in 1st gear: Isabella 40%, TS 42%, Combi 32%

Suspension, Steering, Tires, Brakes
Self-bearing all-steel construction
Independent front suspension
Rear swing axle
Individual pressure lubrication
Front and rear coil springs and telescopic shock absorbers
Hypoid-geared differential
Rear axle ratio 3.9:1
ZF roller-segment steering
Turning circle 11 meters
Tires 5.90 x 13 tubeless
Hydraulic four-wheel brakes
Oversize brake surface 744 square centimeters
Mechanical hand brake

Performance and Consumption
Isabella
Top speed approximately 130 kph
Fuel consumption by DIN 70030 9.1 liters/100 km (Testing speed 98 kph)

Isabella TS, de Luxe, Coupé)
Top speed approximately 150 kph
Fuel consumption by DIN 70030 9.2 liters/100 km (testing speed 110 kph)

Interior
Isabella
Seat width from door to door, front and rear 1.48 meters
Fresh-air heating
Defroster

Isabella TS *)
Combined flat down and felt upholstery
Separate front seats with adjustable backs
Fresh-air heating
Defroster
Standing heating

de Luxe, Coupé)
Combined flat down and foam rubber upholstery
Separate seats with adjustable backs
Fresh-air heating
Defroster
Standing heating
Windshield washer
Flasher lights
Asymmetrical non-glare light

Weights and Measures
Isabella TS, de Luxe
Dry weight approx. 1045 kg
Allowable gross weight approx. 1410 kg
Length 4400 mm
Width 1760 mm
Height 1500 mm unladen
Wheelbase 2600 mm
Front track 1346 mm
Rear track 1370 mm
Ground clearance 175 mm
Coupé
Length 4400 mm
Width 1730 mm
Height 1380 mm unladen
Dry weight approx. 1100 kg
Allowable gross weight approx. 1410 kg
Isabella Combi *)
Dry weight approx. 1130 kg
Allowable gross weight approx. 1700 kg
Interior cargo space:
Length approx. 1580 mm
Width approx. 1400 mm
Height approx. 915 mm
* Variations from the production Isabella sedan

Technische Daten

Motor
4 Zylinder in Reihe
Dreipunktaufhängung in Gummi
Hubvolumen 1493 ccm
Bohrung 75 mm, Hub 84,5 mm
Verdichtung 1:7
60 PS
Max. Drehmoment 11 mkg
mech. Benzinpumpe
Wasserkühlung mit Thermostat und Pumpe
Fallstromvergaser Solex PJCB
Panzerventile hängend
Elektr. Anlage 6 V, Batterie 84 Ah

Isabella TS, de Luxe, Coupé *)
Verdichtung 1:8,2
75 PS
Max. Drehmoment 11,6 mkg
Registervergaser Solex PAJTA

Kupplung und Getriebe
Hydr. Einscheiben-Trockenkupplung
Lenkrad-Schaltung
4 vollsynchr. Vorwärtsgänge
1 Rückwärtsgang
Untersetzungen:
1. Gang 2. Gang 3. Gang 4. Gang
3,86   2,15   1,36   1
Steigfähigkeit im 1. Gang ca. Isabella 40%; TS 42%; Combi 32%

Fahrwerk, Lenkung Reifen, Bremsen
Selbsttragende Ganzstahlkaross.
vorn Einzelradaufhängung
hinten Pendelachse
Einzeldruckschmierung
Vorn und hinten Schraubenfedern und Teleskopstoßdämpfer
hypoidverzahnt. Hinterachsantr.
Untersetzung 1:3,9
ZF-Rollensegment-Lenkung
Wendekreis 11 m
Reifen 5,90x13, schlauchlos
Hydraulische Vierradbremse
Überdimensionierte Bremsfläche 744 qcm
Mechanische Handbremse

Leistung und Verbrauch
Isabella
Spitzengeschwindigkeit ca. 130 km/h
Kraftstoffverbrauch nach DIN 70030 9,1 l/100 km (Prüfgeschwindigkeit 98 km/h)

Isabella TS, de Luxe, Coupé*)
Spitzengeschwindigkeit ca. 150 km/h

Kraftstoffverbrauch nach DIN 70030
9,2 l/100 km (Prüfgeschwindigkeit 110 km/h)

Innenraum
Isabella
Sitzbreite von Tür zu Tür vorn 1,48 m hinten 1,48 m
Frischluft-Heizung
Defroster

Isabella TS*)
kombinierte Flachfeder- und Gummihaarpolster
vorn Einzelsitze mit Schlaflehnen
Frischluft-Heizung
Defroster
Standheizung

de Luxe, Coupé*)
Kombinierte Flachfeder- und Schaumgummipolster
Einzelsitze mit Schlaflehnen
Frischluft-Heizung
Defroster
Standheizung
Scheibenwaschanlage
Lichthupe
asymm. Abblendlicht

Abmessungen und Gewichte
Isabella TS, de Luxe
Leergewicht ca. 1045 kg
zul. Gesamtgewicht ca. 1410 kg
Länge 4400 mm
Breite 1760 mm
Höhe 1500 mm unbel.
Radstand 2600 mm
Spurweite vorn 1346 mm
Spurweite hinten 1370 mm
Bodenfreiheit 175 mm

Coupé*)
Länge 4400 mm
Breite 1730 mm
Höhe 1380 mm unbel.
Leergewicht ca. 1100 kg
zul. Gesamtgewicht ca. 1410 kg

Isabella Combi*)
Leergewicht ca. 1130 kg
zul. Gesamtgewicht ca. 1700 kg
Laderaum:
Länge ca. 1580 mm
Breite ca. 1400 mm
Höhe ca. 915 mm

*) Abweichungen gegenüber der serienmäßigen Isabella-Limousine

A variation of the Isabella sedan was the
convertible with the same basic bodywork.
This vehicle was built by the Cologne firm
of Deutsch. The TS Convertible cost 12,535
Marks and was thus priced about 4000
Marks lower than the 190 SL.

Isabella coupé

Besitzer dieses Wagens haben eigene Maßstäbe.
Von Leistung braucht man nicht zu reden, sie ist
bei einem solchen Automobil selbstverständlich.
Worin liegt sein Wert? In der unnachahmlichen
Eleganz, die sich auf dem Golf-Platz ebenso stilecht
präsentiert, wie bei der Auffahrt zum Opernhaus.

Isabella Coupe

Owners of this car have their own standards. One does not need to
mention performance; it can be taken for granted in such a car.
Wherein is its value? In the inimitable elegance that is just as stylish at
the golf course as at the entrance to the opera house.

LANCIA & C.   ·   *Convertible* AURELIA G. T. 2500

The Lancia has been a particular delicacy for years. The 110-HP Aurelia Spider was produced in small numbers from 1956 to 1959- even then a rare for the aficionado, cherished by the connoisseur.

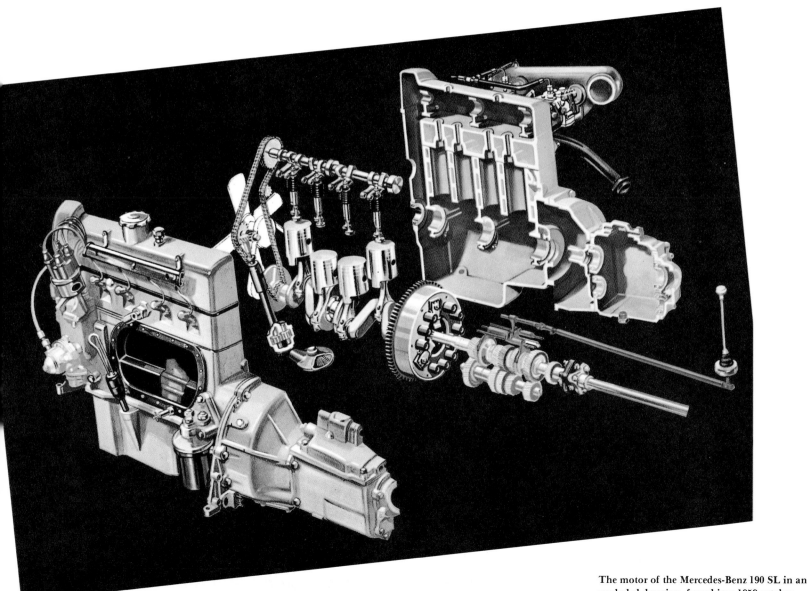

The motor of the Mercedes-Benz 190 SL in an
exploded drawing, found in a 1959 catalog.

This catalog is also a rarity. At that time it was customary-and not just at Daimler-Benz-to use drawings of the vehicles rather than photographs. Talented graphic artists had greater opportunities than photographers, who had problems with color technology, which was not very far advanced at that time.

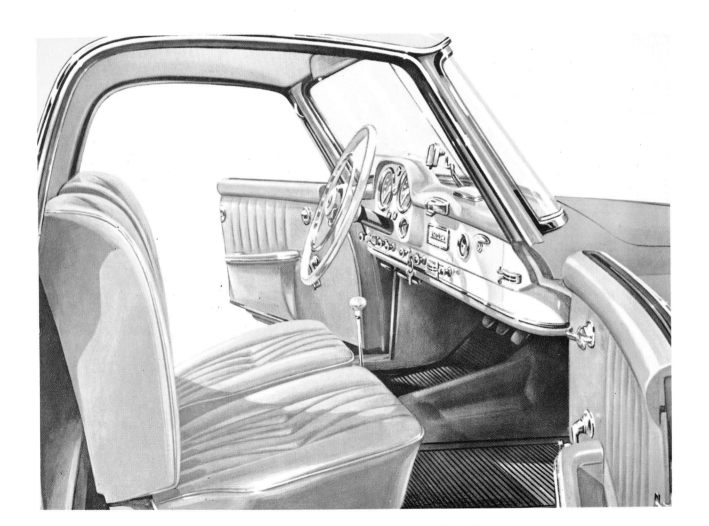

The 190 SL in Miniature

The Mercedes-Benz 190 SL was one of the few automobiles that remained unchanged during their entire production time (1955 to 1963). As a model car, the 190 SL was put on the market chiefly by the manufacturers of sheet metal toys. The miniatures are just as desirable collectors' pieces today as is the real thing. The choice, as our listing shows, is considerable.

Manufacturer	Form	Material	Scale
190 SL Cabriolet			
Anguplas (E)	Readymade	Plastic	1/88
Wiking (D)	Readymade	Plastic	1/87
Eko (E)	Readymade	Plastic	1/86
Lego (Dk)	Readymade	Plastic	1/85
Minicar (Iran)	Readymade	Plastic	1/60 (ex-Siku)
Siku (D)	Readymade	Plastic	1/60
Märklin (D)	Readymade	Diecast	1/45
Dalia-Solido (E)	Readymade	Metal	1/43 (ex-Solido)
Solido (F)	Readymade	Metal	1/43
Tomte (N)	Readymade	Rubber	1/43
Scalextric (GB)	Readymade	Plastic	1/32
Triang Minic (GB)	Readymade	Tinplate	1/32
JNF (D)	Readymade	Tinplate	1/25
Kellermann (D)	Readymade	Tinplate	1/24 (approx.)
Gama (D)	Readymade	Tinplate	1/24 (approx.,Polizei)
Huki (D)	Readymade	Tinplate	1/20 (approx.)
Schuco (D)	Readymade	Tinplate	1/20 (approx.)
Schuco (D)	Readymade	Tinplate	1/20 (approx., Rollyvox)
JNF (D)	Readymade	Tinplate	1/18 (approx.)
190 SL Hardtop			
Schuco Piccolo (D)	Readymade	Metal	1/90
Anguplas (E)	Readymade	Plastic	1/88
Wiking (D)	Readymade	Plastic	1/87
Hammer (D)	Readymade	Plastic	1/87
Eko (E)	Readymade	Plastic	1/86
Dinky-France (F)	Readymade	Metal	1/43
Dinky-France (F)	Readymade	Metal	1/43
Walldorf (D)	Kit	Metal	1/43
Schuco (D)	Readymade	Metal	1/41
Tootsie-Toys (USA)	Readymade	Metal	1/40 (approx.)
Dux (D)	Readymade	Tinplate	1/38
KDN (CS)	Readymade	Tinplate	1/35
JNF (D)	Readymade	Tinplate	1/25 (approx.)
Revell (USA)	Kit	Plastic	1/25
Gama (D)	Readymade	Tinplate	1/24
Gama (D)	Readymade	Tinplate	1/20 (approx.)
Joustra (F)	Readymade	Tinplate	1/20 (approx.)
Schuco (D)	Readymade	Tinplate	1/20 (approx.)
Schuco (D)	Readymade	Tinplate	1/20 (approx., Polizei)

The 190 SL as Seen in the Press

There were no magic photos popping up in the press before the official presentation of the 190 SL; rather there were drawings-and they much resembled the car introduced in New York in February of 1954. In its first January 1954 issue, *Auto, Motor und Sport* published two such sketches, which were strongly reminiscent of the 300 SL, and the photo caption mentioned a 1.6-liter motor, the information said to come from "usually well-informed sources". The Americans, it was reported, were talking of a 1.9-liter

The prototype takes shape in Sindelfingen.

engine, which turned out to be correct. Then came the first official report. The American magazine *Road & Track* described the car in connection with the 300 SL-as did many other journals-and stressed that in the 190 SL "a car was created for the Mercedes fan that conjured up the sensation of the 300 SL but could be bought for less than half the price". The international press spoke of an elegant, fast touring sports car (completely in the spirit of the Mercedes-Benz press releases) that could be used as a utilitarian everyday vehicle but also in "sporting events of a lesser nature" (*Auto, Motor und Sport*). The car, by

Above: the complete chassis with motor installed in the front sub-frame. The profile members were welded to the bottom sheets.

Right: The trunk of the 190 SL.

Opposite page: Final assembly on the assembly line. In the background is a gull-wing 300 SL.

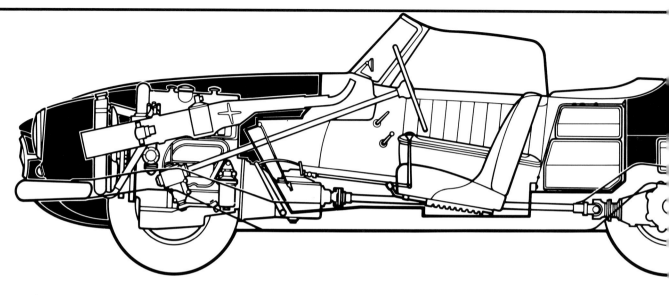

no means ready for series production, was still to be changed in numerous ways before it went into production in May of 1955. The two "box seats" that were to be an option instead of the one-piece bench-type seat, remained nothing but an advertising idea. Nor was the 190 SL built to be a racing sports car, the roadster version without lowering windows left the Stuttgart factory only seven or eight times. "A model was shown to the Highest National Sport Commission (ONS) in 1955," wrote Winfried A. Seidel in the 1982 *Automobil Chronik*. "To be sure, the roadster top had been installed in this car, and in order to be able to attach the top, the car also had the large, arched windshield."

Although the official ONS auto-test journal stated in addition, "Variations are allowed, insofar as the technical data of the car are not changed by them, only through the utilization of original production parts for the model in question, delivered by the manufacturing factory", there were immediate

protests when the Mercedes-Benz 190 SL appeared in a "racing version".

Winfried A. Seidel wrote: "At their meeting in Paris, the FIA decided in February of 1956 not to allow the Mercedes-Benz 190 SL with the small racing windshield and lighter roadster doors to compete in the GT category. The cars thus modified were limited to the production sports car class, where they had a slim chance. In fact, even removing the bumpers was banned if the 190 SL's were to run in the grand touring class. When the 190 Sport SL was shown to the ONS, it had its bumpers in place . . .

"In a memo sent by Racing Director Alfred Neubauer to the various involved departments at the Daimler-Benz works on March 3, 1956, he referred to this situation and suggested that all references to the third version of the 190 SL be removed from further advertisements. He also recommended that the car no longer be sold to German customers in the version with "small windshield and light doors". All those who had already bought the car in this version, Neubauer continued, should be informed of the new FIA decision by the customer service department, so that no one would be in danger of being banned.

Cutaway drawing of the Mercedes-Benz 190 SL, made by Siegfried Werner. Clear to see is the very useful luggage space behind the seats. There was a special set of suitcases for this car.

"That was, at least for Europe, the early death of the racing 190 SL. But there were still a few racing entries, even successful ones, outside Europe, for example in Asia. Inquiries brought to light that two cars had been used for racing by the Zung Fu Daimler-Benz agency in Hong Kong. One of the cars took second place overall, and won its class, in the 1956 Grand Prix of the Portuguese colony of Macão.

"Another sporting victory was the class win in the 1958 Hong Kong Rally. And, in 1961 a racing SL in which a Type OM 621 Diesel engine had been installed was driven to Diesel records."

A look at the 105-HP motor of the 190 SL. Everything is remarkably easy to reach-a matter of good spacing.

Above is a hardtop roadster without chrome ornamentation. At right is the special model equipped for racing (New York, 1954).

Naturally the 190 SL was anything but a "racing car". Its qualities were in another area. Comfort and safety came first, as the testers of *The Autocar* confirmed. But they also praised the car's temperament, "105 HP is a remarkable achievement for a 1.9-liter motor . . . one must just shift busily, especially on the highway. In fourth gear, at 175 kph, there is still a lot of power." One could understand the need for a lot of shifting, since a motor of this size, which could reach 6000 rpm, could not be particularly flexible. The car's cold starting was also impressive, "It started immediately when the choke was pulled and then immediately pushed back in, otherwise a warning light came on. If one gave a relatively cold motor full gas too soon, it caused misfiring."

The motor was called a masterpiece by many testers. "Under the hood of the 180 many imagined a cut-off 220 motor before it materialized," it was written in *Auto, Motor und Sport*, "but nothing came of it. Now the dream has more or less come true in the 190 SL. Its motor is built by the principles of the Types 220 and 300; one might even call it a cut-down 300 motor, with which it corresponds exactly in the bore (85 mm) and almost in the stroke (83.6 mm as opposed to 88 mm in the 300). The 1897-cc four-cylinder motor with single overhead camshaft and two horizontal carburetors produced 110 HP by German norms and 125 HP by those of the SAE, giving the car, which weighs 1050 kg ready to drive, a top speed of 190 kph (129 kph in third gear). The fully synchronized four-speed gearbox with stick shift is the same as that of the Type 180."

Five years after it went into production, the 190 SL was examined again by the same journal. But it had become difficult to judge the car fairly, it still had all its previous weaknesses, but on the other hand it enjoyed such great popularity that it "will probably continue to be built for a long time, since the demand rather increases than decreases", which obviously had been expected by the magazine writers.

"Although it is not exactly cheap, the 190 SL had attained a popularity that puts it in a class with other fast-selling sports cars such as the MG, Triumph, Jaguar, Alfa Romeo Giulietta or Porsche types. More than 18,000 190 SL cars had left the factory since 1955.

"Of course it seems to be a very particular public that prefers the 190 SL. Its popularity in motion pictures, as a background in fashion magazines, the frequency of its being seen in the hands of stars of the most various types show the direction, not always to the unqualified pleasure of its manufacturers. But there is no doubt that the 190 SL is more at home on the boulevard than on the race track. That is part of its nature."

The car's elegance suits the need to brag "inborn in all of us", Reinhard Seiffert wrote. Its styling "shows that its creators were very sensitive to the external effect of a sporting car." The 190 SL drew jealous as well as admiring, coquettish as well as inviting looks to itself . . .

But, said Seiffert, one should not feel superior about it, for in the end, everybody would like to go for a ride in a beautiful open car, and then too, the 190 SL was after all a Mercedes, "the Star of Stuttgart enjoys an extraordinary esteem among the world's trade marks." Undoubtedly the car with the star guarantees quality, and so the 190 SL had a remarkable lot of external attributes that the car could claim for itself and its owner. "The car is famous for not being built to break down; it was not one of those cars that constantly require a tender hand and a good repair shop".

"One has it checked now and then, that is all. That may not seem sensational to owners of ordinary cars. But for sports-car buyers in a country like the United States, where the manufacturer and usually even the nearest authorized service agency, are far away, it is

Coupe and Roadster, model year 1958.

not at all taken for granted and is highly appreciated. That is why the Americans value the 190 SL."

The open roadster was preferred by *Auto, Motor und Sport,* it was stated in issue 15 of 1960-the car was particularly enjoyable to drive with the top down. And: "The body is not only pretty, but also of outstanding quality. One notices the precise closing of the doors or the front and rear hoods, just as in small details such as the solidly built locking door of the glove compartment and the excellent interior furnishings. The construction and external appearance of the 190 SL still earn a grade of A today."

John Christy, test driver for *Sports Cars Illustrated,* wrote in 1958: "Whoever sits in the 190 SL has a definite need to drive fast. That is a tangible pleasure; the car seems to come alive. As the speed increases, the steering becomes lighter, the gas can be given precisely, and even the sounds stay within limits-one hears only the humming of the motor. This humming offers a taste of living!" His only reservation referred to the speedometer. In his test car it was 6 miles (10 km) fast at its top speed of 109 MPH . . .

His German colleagues in Stuttgart criticized the limited lateral support of the seats and the not overly efficient shock absorbers. And, "Despite its good roadhandling, fast cornering with the 190 SL is rather exhausting". This was attributed to three causes: "First of all, the steering, while not exactly heavy, has a very high recoil power, because of which the steering wheel must be held quite firmly. Second, on a rough road the bumps in the pavement are felt in the steering column and wheel, so that the hands cannot rest. And third, the seats offer too little lateral support, so that one cannot brace himself with his body while steering but has to hold fast to the steering wheel. Thus the 190 SL behaves less smoothly than one is accustomed to in a sports car, and one feels little urge to force it on its way for a long time. When one drives it with the top down-during the test period we ample opportunity to do so in warm summer weather-one is not so sensitive to this; top-down driving is simply fun all the time-even though a little self-delusion is involved, for one always feels faster than one is."

To sum up: "The 190 SL is hard to judge, because it is certainly not a bad car . . . driving safety, roadhandling, performance are unobjectionable, body and workmanship are outstanding." But is that all that one expects of a sports car from the house of Daimler-Benz in 1960? It was a nice robust automobile, but by 1955 standards, "Even with the best intentions, it can no longer inspire enthusiasm."

That was 1960. And it still remained in the program, unchanged, until February of 1963. Then the enthusiasm really decreased-or transferred to its successor. The 190 SL was only rediscovered some time later, as a favorite of devoted Mercedes fans who track down all surviving examples in order to preserve them and restore them through painstaking labor.

190 SL-Technical Data

Motor

Four-cylinder in-line motor
Bore x stroke 85 x 83.6 mm, displacement 1897 cc
Compression ratio 8.5:1 (as of September 1959 8.8:1)
Horsepower: 105 DIN HP at 5700 rpm
Torque: 14.5 mkg at 3200 rpm
Single overhead camshaft driven by duplex chain
Crankshaft with three main bearings
Cooling by water (10 liters)
Lubrication: pressure lubrication with mainstream oil filter and oil cooler (4 liters)
2 Solex 44 PHH horizontal carburetors
Battery: 12-volt 16 Ah.
Generator: 160 W

Transmission

Single-plate dry clutch
Four-speed gearbox with stick shift
Gear ratios: 1. 3.52, 2. 2.32, 3. 1.52, 4. 1.00, reverse 3.29
Rear axle ratio: 3.90
Power transmission to the rear wheels by half-shafts

Body

Self-bearing sheet steel construction welded to frame-bottom unit

Suspension

Front: independent suspension by double transverse links with coil springs and stabilizer
Rear: single-link swing axle with push struts and coil springs Telescopic oleopneumatic shock absorbers

Steering

Recirculating ball, 18.5:1, with steering damper, 3.5 revolutions from stop to stop

Brakes

Hydraulically activated drum brakes, front duplex, diameter 230 mm, total braking surface: 1064 cc
Optional servo power brakes ATE T 50 (standard as of 1956)
Hand brake by cables to the rear wheels

Weights and Measures

Wheels: sheet steel disc wheels, 5 K x 13
Tires: 6.40-13 sport
Wheelbase: 2400 mm
Track: front 1430 mm, rear 1475 mm
Ground clearance: 155 mm
Length x width x height: 4220 x 1740 x 1320 mm
Dry weight: 1080 kg, hardtop: 20 kg
Allowable gross weight: 1400 kg, as of 1961: 1440 kg
Top speed: approximately 170 kph
Fuel consumption: approx. 12.5 liters of premium gas per 100 km
Number made from May 1955 to February 1963: 25,881
Prices: Roadster with convertible top—DM 16,500
Coupe with removable top—DM 17,100
Coupe/Roadster with hardtop and convertible top—DM 17,650

Mercedes-Benz Literature (190 SL)

Much has been written about Mercedes automobiles, not only on the occasion of the hundredth anniversary of this, the world's oldest brand of automobiles. But few of these books contain anything exhaustive about the 190 SL. Here is a short list of the appropriate titles.

Mercedes-Benz Automobile. This five-volume Mercedes typology by Halwart Schrader and Herbert Hofner examines all production models and their experimental versions and special equipment. Every model is described, technically documented and illustrated in detail. Outstanding photographic material, excellently reproduced. The 190 SL is the subject of a thoroughgoing description in Volume 4, with all technical details. 168 pages, approx. 260 black-and-white photos and 16 pages in color.

Mercedes-Benz Cars 1957-61, a volume in the Brooklands Series (English text), containing reprints from American and English journals. Two articles treat the 190 SL. 100 pp, A4.

Mercedes-Benz Personenwagen 1886-1986, by Werner Oswald. This unique book offers an inclusive overview of all passenger cars produced by Daimler and Benz in the past hundred years. 680 pages, 1300 illustrations.

Mercedes for the Road, by Henry Rasmussen. A splendid photo volume by this unique photographer, in the universally acclaimed Survivors Series. The following models are portrayed: 220A Convertible, 300Sc Roadster, 300ST Coupe, 300 SL Roadster, 190 SL Roadster, 300d Sedan, 220 SE Convertible, 600 Limousine of model years 1969 and 1979. 135 pages, 173 illustrations, 164 of them in color. English text.

Mercedes-Benz Catalogue Raisonné. A two-volume encyclopedia with all technical and historical data. 840 pages in all, more than 1000 illustrations, 40 pages in color, German/English/French text.

Mercedes Aust Classics 3: Mercedes 190 SL, edited by Stefan Knittel. A well-compiled typology with many good black-and-white and color photos. 48 pages, approx. 60 illustrations, a double page in color. English/German text.

Sterne, Stars und Majestäten-Prominenz auf Mercedes-Benz, by P. Simsa and J. Lewandowski. This book shows in text and many pictures how generations have been fascinated by the car with the "star". 160 pages, 230 black-and-white photographs.

Mercedes 190 SL. Reprint of the service directions. A5, WK 491.

Mercedes 190 SL. Reprint of the spare parts list, more than 300 pages, A5 WK 870.

Mercedes-Benz Clubs

Mercedes-190-SL-Club, U. H. Larkamp,
Rheingaustrasse 40, D-6802 Ladenburg, West Germany

Mercedes-190-SL-Club,
Oberwaldstrasse 63, D-7500 Karlsruhe 41, West Germany

Mercedes-Veteranen-Club Deutschland e.V.,
Rheingaustrasse 21, D-6802 Ladenburg, West Germany

Bonner Mercedes Veteranen-Club,
P.O. Box 530, D-5300 Bonn, West Germany.

Schweizer Mercedes Veteranen-Club,
G. Bürgin, Hegi 242, CH-4625 Oderbuchsiten, Switzerland

Club Mercedes-Benz de France,
32 rue Docteur Mercier, F-01130 Nantua, France

Mercedes-SL-Club Austria,
P.O. Box 201, A-1013 Vienna, Austria

Mercedes SL Club, John Olsson,
2020 Girard Street, South Minneapolis MN 55405, USA

Mercedes-Benz Club Ltd.,
The Firs, Biscombe, Churchstanton, Taunton, Somerset TA3 7PZ, England

The cockpit of the
Mercedes-Benz 190 SL in
series production (above)
and that of the prototype,
which was designed as a
competition car. The
cutout doors have no
raising windows, in the
best roadster tradition.